Other titles by the author

NOVELS

Sonata in F-Minor ISBN 978-1-877513-32-9
Trilogy: The Flower of Life:
Vol. I: In the Claws of Sheer Insanity ISBN 978-1-877572-80-7
Vol. II: Recognition of Emptiness ISBN 978-1-877572-75-3
Vol. III: Towards Eternity ISBN 978-1-877572-72-7

TRAVEL BOOKS

Antarctic Revelations ISBN 978-1-877449-70-3
Reflections Down Under ISBN 978-1-877479-48-9

SELF DEVELOPMENT

Echoes of Affirmations ISBN 978-1-877513-71-8

MEDITATION: Pictorial Impressions Books

Antarctic Impressions ISBN 978-1-877479-49-6
Arbour Impressions ISBN 978-1-877526-80-8
Beach Impressions ISBN 978-1-877534-56-0
ClipArt—Witty Impressions ISBN 978-0-473-16212-2
Floral Impressions ISBN 978-1-877526-79-4
Lake Impressions ISBN 978-1-877534-54-6
New Zealand Impressions ISBN 978-1-877513-48-0
Peak Impressions ISBN 978-1-877534-53-9
South Island Impressions ISBN 978-1-877513-41-8
Whispering Waters ISBN 978-1-877534-55-3

Visit *www.booksbyeve.co.nz*

RE-spect

Who Deserves It?

By Eve Linn

BALBOA
PRESS
A DIVISION OF HAY HOUSE

www.booksbyeve.co.nz

Balboa Press books may be ordered through booksellers or by contacting:

Balboa Press
A Division of Hay House
1663 Liberty Drive
Bloomington, IN 47403
www.balboapress.com.au
1-(877) 407-4847

ISBN: 978-1-4525-0397-4 (sc)
ISBN: 978-1-4525-0398-1 (e)

Because of the dynamic nature of the Internet, any web addresses or links contained in this book may have changed since publication and may no longer be valid. The views expressed in this work are solely those of the author and do not necessarily reflect the views of the publisher, and the publisher hereby disclaims any responsibility for them.

The author of this book does not dispense medical advice or prescribe the use of any technique as a form of treatment for physical, emotional, or medical problems without the advice of a physician, either directly or indirectly. The intent of the author is only to offer information of a general nature to help you in your quest for emotional and spiritual well-being. In the event you use any of the information in this book for yourself, which is your constitutional right, the author and the publisher assume no responsibility for your actions.

Any people depicted in stock imagery provided by Thinkstock are models, and such images are being used for illustrative purposes only.
Certain stock imagery © Thinkstock.

Printed in the United States of America

Balboa Press rev. date: 03/30/2012

DON'T YOU DARE

"Don't you dare,"
they said, "to grow,"
and I obeyed.

Swim with the flow,
and you are fine.

All they said
was just a lie,
and I believed.

I did not know
my silent cry.

"Don't you dare,"
they said, "to feel
the sorrows of your heart,"
and I believed—
I really tried,
as I remember,
very hard.

One night,
I saw a face,
and it was mine.

The tears felt soft,
and I felt loved.

I grew from there—
began to share
the feelings in my life.
I dared a lot,
I really did;
my life began to shine.

"Don't you dare,"
I hear them say.
What do they know?
No shine will come from there . . .

(Eve Linn, 08.07.1996)

FOREWORD

Many books are out there for people who are interested in self-development and therapy courses so they can learn more about them. And many of these books undoubtedly appeal to the many interested readers. But I have not come across a book yet which looks at the *values* of respect. We find the term as we grow up in all sorts of authoritarian confrontations, but have we, in fact, ever known or been taught what it means to respect oneself and each other? I have come to doubt that we have. I also wonder whom, in fact, we owe respect to—who or what deserves respect.

Each day in our local, national, and international news we hear about aggressive behaviours and disrespectful actions. Somebody has beaten somebody else up, somebody has killed someone else over a quarrel, property is stolen from a stranger or a friend, and children are bullying children. And it is not happening any longer elsewhere—it's happening on the front steps of our doors. In this context, I also wonder about the fact that these aggressive behaviours might coincide with the recent increasingly disastrous behaviour of Mother Nature. Is it coincidence, or do we need to look deeper?

Something is not quite right. It seems we have, in fact, no knowledge of respect. And what, in its essence, is respect? With the help of this book, I will research the origin of respect and will define the meaning within its day-to-day occurrences. At the end of this book, I also offer a solution, just in case this journey will make this viable.

I am as excited about this journey as you, the readers, are. I have only just started.

So let's go on with it.

Eve Linn
August, 2011

INDEX

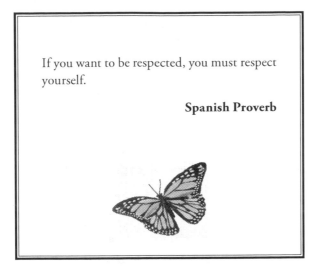

If you want to be respected, you must respect yourself.

Spanish Proverb

DEFINITION OF RESPECT

The *American Heritage Dictionary* (AHD) explains the term "respect" as a transitive verb and noun. As a transitive verb in use, we know respect as "respected," "respecting," or "respects" in the context that one feels or shows deferential regard for somebody or something, even for a cause or an action. The term "deferential" in itself can be understood in many ways depending on which culture we grow up in (e.g., respectful, admiring, reverent, polite, courteous, or obsequious).

The AHD also refers to the term "esteem," which has different cultural ways of expression, such as regard, respect, admiration, high regard, good opinion, value, appreciation, and last but not least, prize. The AHD furthermore explains the verb "respect" as an action—to avoid violation of or interference with somebody or something—and gives the example of respecting a speed limit. In the context of being concerned with somebody or something, the AHD adds that relating to or referring to somebody or something can indicate a respective approach. As a noun, the AHD shows the following examples to illustrate the term "respect":

1. A feeling of appreciative, often deferential regard; esteem. See Synonyms at regard.
2. The state of being regarded with honour or esteem.
3. Willingness to show consideration or appreciation.
4. Polite expressions of consideration or deference: pay one's respects.

What becomes obvious is the connection "respect" has with esteem, appreciation, honour, and regard. I would like to look into the etymology of the term "respect" to understand the evolution of this word's usage.

If we look at the Latin verb *respicere,* we are told that it means simply "looking back at" or "regarding," whereas the verb *respecere* in the Indo-European proto-language means "looking at." With one little letter change from *I* to *E* in *respicere* to *respecere,* we already can find a different way of culturally employing these words.

But the term "respect" also offers a unique use—the highlighting of something special. For instance, we use the term as a detail—a point or characteristic in saying, "She differs in some respects from her daughters." In other words, "She is unique," and it is this very uniqueness that I would like to draw attention to. In my understanding, respect carries a value of uniqueness.

Our society has become a pluralistic, economic society, and individuality—*uniqueness*—has become less appreciated for the simple reason that it cannot drive a wealthy society. A wealthy society does need plural members; one unique person alone simply cannot establish a wealthy industry. Industry in the days following WWII promised a more comfortable lifestyle. In my understanding, this is the core of the evil. Money speaks louder than actions. More to the point, it is louder than respect.

The Free Online Dictionary (FOD) shows an example of the usage of the term "respect" in regard to estimation or an estimate, the respect with which a person is held, and gives the following example: "They had a high estimation of his ability." This statement reminds me of the very esteemed tradition of labour and trade.

My childhood in West Germany was filled with respect for labour and trade, hard workers, and skilled tradesmen. Back then, esteem was very much associated with the adjectives "hard" and "skilled," not with the nouns "workers" and "tradesmen." Workers and tradesmen alike had to earn their respect. And it was with this value that the meaning of "prize," as explained in the AHD, could grow from, as we literally came to prize the skilfulness of a tradesman as well as the hardship of a labourer.

Values of esteem and respect started to change greatly within the twentieth century. Industrialization, new technologies, farming with the goal of import/export, and automation shifted a great part of the world's population toward fiscal values. The hardworking dollar changed into a figure on a balance sheet. In other words, where we once could *respicere*— or in the Indo-European proto-language, *respecere*—during the last half of the twentieth century, we now could no longer look at our weekly wages in our hands. Instead, we gained a bank account and a balance sheet. We had lost our ability to see the value of our labour and trade.

Hence, the following generation lost the ability to *respicere/respecere*, the value of its own (individual, unique) work. Respect had gone out of our hands and into a bank account and was not owned anymore—it was out of view, so to speak. It could not be looked back at, let alone looked at. Instead, with a bank account and black figures on a white paper, greed and power grew. Respect was not earned anymore; it was paid and looked at on a sheet of paper. And the more one could see in one's bank account, the more one seemed to grow in terms of esteem in society. We can see how respect and esteem seemed to have grown apart.

The FOD also speaks of respect in the context of attitude—the mental state involving beliefs, feelings, values, and dispositions to act in certain ways. For example, "He had the attitude that work was fun." It seems obvious that attitudes with a changed lifestyle will also change. A population that is driven by pluralistic values will automatically change away from individual values, as they do not support the success of their society. The mental state of a pluralistic, economic society is a complex fragment of its own desires, and individual, unique needs have to be left behind. Uniqueness does not pay. Pluralism does. Consequently, the value of the "I" has shifted to the value of the "we." A "we" mental state, though, is hardly genuine or liveable. It offers avenues towards anonymity, conformism, and last but not least, a fake patriotism or religion.

The FOD furthermore links respect to a courteous expression, by word or deed, of esteem or regard and gives the following examples: "His deference to her wishes was very flattering" or "Be sure to give my respect to the dean." Reading this, I hardly can remember when this kind of deference has been given to me or when I would have witnessed such displayed respect elsewhere in my life in recent years. I do see a lot of disrespect, though, and I have come to wonder if again a pluralistic economic society can be blamed for the vanishing of courteous expressions. I have not seen many acts of showing regard for others—not in my neighbourhood, not at theatre performances, not in movies, or at any other public events.

That brings me to the biblical admonition in the fifth of the Ten Commandments: "Honour your father and your mother, that your days may be long upon the land which the Lord your God is giving you." [1] It clearly commands you to respect your parents in the context of your days upon the land. In the pluralistic, economic society of today, we do not have our days upon the land; even for farmers, the land has become a business resource. Even though I respect the Ten Commandments as a valuable guideline to live by, I will not go too deeply into this religious edict concerning the value of respect at this point. But we will discuss the influence of a religious society later on in the book.

I have always wondered how we can respect our parents when they have not earned the respect as such. But children of any kind of upbringing—be it kind or abusive—are told to pay respect to their parents. Again, there is a price to pay to become regarded. Respect towards parents these days, I feel, has changed to an emphasis on pleasing them. Children have learnt to adapt their behaviour to please their parents. How many children have later chosen a career to please their parents rather than fulfilling their own career wishes? How often do we hear the words, "It was his filial duty to become a farmer, too"? That, certainly, did not honour this pleasing boy's uniqueness. Such a boy might have become an extraordinary mechanic, researcher, bookkeeper, lawyer, or even a writer or essayist. Who knows?

Also, the respect—as an action of pleasing—shown towards parents nowadays can be seen as a learnt skill of obedience, which in my opinion throws the essence of respect completely out of its cradle. The only matter that is being looked back at or looked at in this context is the authority of the parental figure, irrespective of parental actions. In certain situations, obedience can be rather vital, and as such, I respect the ability to be obedient as well as the adage of "do as you are told." As long as obedience serves a good intention—let's say to protect, safeguard, or enforce something—I can without any hesitation accept a necessity for it. In certain careers, obedience is an absolute must. But I fail to link obedience with the true meaning of respect. To the contrary, I believe too much exercised obedience lets respect again go out of its cradle of origin.

But there is an area where I still see respect displayed today, and it is often very genuinely shown. This is on the occasion of funerals when one pays respect to the deceased. It is a very enlightened feeling for me to find somebody standing quietly at the graveside of a deceased family member, friend, or colleague to pay his or her last respects. It would be very nice to see this quietness and, in a way, solitude at the side of a family member, friend, or colleague whilst that person is still alive. That to me would bring respect back into our lifestyle. But we have forgotten how to be quiet and how to be private with somebody else around. A pluralistic, economy-driven society cannot live like that. A pluralistic economic society has bred noisy, hectic people—doers rather than "be-ers." And in that, we also have learnt to misunderstand signs of affection, warmth, fondness, or tenderness, which of course, all could be part of a respectful approach.

How often do women mistake one's manly regard for love, for instance? Power and greed can lead to extreme loneliness and neediness, and if one's affection comes your way, you will be surprised and helpless, not knowing how to deal with such warmth, appreciation, and respect. I can see this phenomenon quite often in adolescents. Of course, this phenomenon works vice versa, with manly regard or womanly regard. Unfortunately, this very lack of self-respect (self-*respecere*—being able to look back at yourself or simply at yourself) has led to inconceivable acts of abuse and violence. Often a child who is not respected for who and what he or she is becomes a victim. A victim is only too eager to be used and abused; everything for a little bit of attention becomes the rule of life. But let's face it—attention is, by far, miles away from respect.

New Zealand has the highest suicide rate among adolescents in the world. I am in awe of how this little country at the end of the world could become a pluralistic economic society in such a short time of existence, quickly following the rules of power and greed and ignoring the uniqueness of personality in its children.

In no other country have I witnessed how the matters of work are manipulating people like dancing dolls within their lifestyle to the extent that the lifestyle in fact gets lost. People in New Zealand don't go to work. People in New Zealand earn a dollar. The ethics around work seem to have gone astray in this country.

I can still see these ethics in the elder generation—the labourers and skilled tradesmen. They do still display respect, consideration, and courtesy. But the later following generation, which shies away from going to work and instead earns a dollar, doesn't seem to know what respect is.

So let's dive a little deeper.

> The way to procure insults is to submit to them: a man meets with no more respect than he exacts.
>
> **William Hazlitt (1778-1830)**

RESPECT TOWARDS FAMILY MEMBERS

We spoke of the Fifth Commandment before: "Honour your father and your mother, that your days may be long upon the land which the Lord your God is giving you."

This always has confused me deeply. How can I, as a newborn child in a completely strange world born to equally strange parents upon their land, *respecere* what is before me? Isn't it obvious that respect has to be taught—in other words, seen or looked at? Isn't it the responsibility of a mother and/or a father to look at me as a newborn first so that I can learn what it means to be looked at? Isn't that how the pathway of respect and acknowledgment has to start in one's life? I wonder . . .

I and Thou is a book by Martin Buber that was published in 1923. Buber suggested that we may address existence in two ways. One is that of the "I" towards an "it"—that is, towards an object that is separate in itself, which we even as newborns either use or experience. The second way is that of the "I" towards "thou," in which we move into existence in a relationship without bounds. Martin Buber concludes that human life finds its meaning in relationships. All of our relationships, says Buber, bring us ultimately into a relationship with God—the eternal "thou." [2]

For Buber, there are two pairs of words for two fundamentally different types of relationship—the "I—it" and the "I—thou" relationship. Whatever the "it" might be—an entity as a discrete object which makes it evidently different from other living entities, like Mum and Dad or brother and sister—this "it" is in a person's life. And this is also what the newborn will perceive. But the "I—thou" relationship is a separate concept. The "I" in this relationship is sustained in the spirit and mind of an "I—thou" for however long the feeling or idea of relationship is the dominant mode of perception. Buber explains, for instance, that a person sitting next to a complete stranger on a park bench may enter into an "I—thou" relationship with the stranger merely by beginning to think positively about people in general. The stranger is a person as well, obviously, and gets instantaneously drawn into a mental or spiritual relationship with the person whose positive thoughts necessarily include the stranger as a member of the set of persons about whom positive thoughts are directed. In this spiritual connection, however, it is not necessary for the stranger to have any idea that he is being drawn into an "I—thou" relationship for such a relationship to arise. My understanding of this "I—thou" example is that the stranger easily could be the newborn and the "thou" the parents.

Let's now examine if young parents, when looking at their newborn, are able to have positive thoughts of people in general that emerge in the very presence of the newborn. Most parents I have witnessed did not at all think of other people in general at that moment in time, when looking at their newborn for the very first time. They thought of the miracle of having such a beautiful baby and that their baby was the most beautiful of all. Yet the newborn is still very untouched from conditioning and knows little of the make-up of a society, let alone of economy or pluralism. The baby will only initially perceive its "I" within the context of the "I—thou" relationship and will pick up the energy of its parents as its reality "upon the land," on which all participants are residing and acting next to the newborn.

The "I" will initially only grow through the "I—thou" connection—a very strong attachment—as a newborn has not yet established a recognition of "I" in itself. The "I" of the newborn is bounded by others—"it"s and "thou"s—and will learn that for every object, there is another object. The "thou," though—the parents in this example—has no limitations. When "thou"—the parents—is spoken, the speaker has nothing, which means that "thou" is abstract. The speaker takes his stand in relation.

How will a newborn experience the world? It will notice that humankind goes around the world, hauling out knowledge from the world. But these experiences, the newborn will soon learn, present humankind with mere words of "it," "he," "she," and "it" with contrast to "I—thou." And this newborn learner will then learn that experiences are all physical yet do involve a great deal of spirituality. Consequently, the twofold nature of the world means that our experience of the world has two aspects: the aspect of experience, which is experienced by the "I—it" relationship, and the aspect of relation, which is perceived by the "I—thou."

It becomes obvious that the newborn needs to perceive a sense of respect for humankind (that is, consequently, from it) to grow into one person who then can give out respectful thoughts in his or her environment later on, as well. Love in itself, according to Buber, is a subject relationship—that is, an "I—it" relationship. Like the "I—thou" relationship, love is not a relationship of subject to object, but rather a relationship in which both members in the relationship are subjects and share the unity of being. In this, the "I—it" becomes a "being—being" relationship.

As I mentioned previously, the ultimate "thou" for Buber is God—or as I prefer to say, creation or existence itself, in which there are no barriers. This then means that man can relate directly to God or creation respectively. Though today's metaphysical approach of understanding life in its essence confirms Buber's teachings, it is by no means widely practiced. God—respectively, creation and existence—is ever-present in human consciousness and manifests itself in music, literature, and other forms of culture. I might add that it even manifests in creating new life within the creation of human life. We must not forget that the newborn is, in fact, part of the same consciousness.

But times have changed. Industrialization, automation, the need for ownership and power, and the need for speed and improvement all have sent different thoughts to our newborns. The "I—thou" relationship has turned into an "it—it" one—that is, the "object—object" relationship. After all, in today's pluralistic societies, we are all mere resources, numbers—ultimately "it"s. The newborn will consequently become a resource and a number for the benefit of a pluralistic economic society in which individuality has no value any longer. Acknowledgment of the self and respect are on the way out.

I would now also look at the essence of respect in regard to authenticity, with which any newborn is truly equipped. In order to keep this authenticity, the newborn would need to feel valued for who she or he is. After all, self-respect is about who we are, not what we do. A baby girl needs to be valued for being a girl; a baby boy needs to be valued for being a boy. Only then can she or he grow into one who can stand tall and feel proud of and for itself simply because it exists. Yes, ultimately the essence of respect in the context of authenticity is about loving ourselves for ourselves. It is easy to see the complications of such development in a pluralistic environment that values a bank account more than anything else.

Despite the fifth commandment, "Honour your father and your mother, that your days may be long upon the land which the Lord your God is giving you," we in the Western and Christian-guided world also learnt according to Mark 12:31 as per the *New Living Translation* of 2007,

"'Love your neighbour as yourself.' No other commandment is greater than these.'"

This commandment has received so many interpretations that one can easily get lost in them. For a long time, I learnt to understand that I had to love my neighbour more than myself; the "as yourself" completely vanished in those interpretations. By the time we go to religion classes in school or are allowed to accompany our parents to church, we already have grown into very pleasing role models of sons and daughters, and we also have learnt that we are loved because of something—the way we look, dress up, communicate (or not), act as pupils, do things, etc.—but most likely not for who we are. The role modelling has taken place from very early on. A newborn develops into a girl and later into a woman, then into a mother, and then maybe into a teacher or nurse—maybe even into a builder in more modern times. But these are all role models which are there to satisfy the needs in a pluralistic, economy-driven society, which is busy educating—if we are lucky—its resources (that is, us human beings) towards its main target. This target is to create a healthy, wealthy, and respectful society.

In this context, let's remember Confucius. Let's also draw attention to the point that Confucius was living in pre-Christian times—that is, 551-479 BC. He was a Chinese thinker and philosopher of the Chinese Spring and Autumn Period. This specific period in China was an age of regional cultures, encroachments, and reforms. From these colourful times of change in China, Confucius wrote his famous words: "Respect yourself, and others will respect you."

In this understanding, self-respect becomes the cornerstone on which many other attributes can be built. These attributes would mainly be honesty, confidence, and integrity. One's sense of self-value and self-respect undoubtedly starts at birth. From then on, self-value and self-respect are forged throughout childhood. It also becomes apparent that it is through the unconditionally loving arms of our mums and dads that we first come in touch with our sense of self-value. The word "touch" is the most important in this context, as that is how babies learn—through touch and not though verbal teachings. All newborns come into this world with basic needs—a need for touch, food, expression, and exploring. It is vital that needs are immediately met. The immediate response to the baby's need is vital for its learning of its value in life. At this time, it does not matter if the baby is a *she* or a *he*. The needs of both genders are equally important.

We also know by now that our newborns—even at a time prior to birth—do sense mum's energy as being positive or negative, free-spirited or burdened. The baby will bring this knowledge into its life. This becomes an integrated part of the baby's "I—thou" relationship. Looking at the pure innocence of a newborn always brings the words to me that everything in life indeed loops around loving ourselves for ourselves simply because we *are*. We only have to remember or *respecere* (look back) some years ago, when we have been at the same place and space in time as a newborn.

How often do you hear—and it does not matter if you hear it from a man or a woman—"It is always easier for me to take care of others and to see their wants and needs than to recognize and see my own"? Be honest— how often per week do you hear this statement? With these statements, it is also obvious that most likely, none of us have been taught the essential meaning of the fifth commandment or of Confucius.

Well, look back; when you were that newborn, did you receive immediate attention for your needs? Do you still remember the unconditionally loving arms of your mother or father, siblings, or grandparents? Do you remember a free-spirited energy around you or a burdened one?

Life in general—from the first day onward—impacts us and forces us to make decisions about how we should respect ourselves. Any "should" is a demand of a society that makes pluralism and economy its principal foundation for existence. It is not a demand from an unconditionally loving parent. Yes, in many ways, we are told—not taught—how love and esteem should look and how we could recognize it when it approaches us. Those "should" impact all of us. We are, consequently, most likely losing our authenticity in this process. Chances are that our public respect will increase but our self-respect will cease. Again, it becomes transparent how our genuine self, from early on, receives knocks and bruises. A pluralistic economic society mainly has a pessimistic and judgemental nature. A glass is always half empty and "should" be filled again.

As a parent, I could teach my newborn of a beautiful-looking glass that is half full. That could indeed be a very simple, optimistic approach from which the child will learn that a half-full glass is richer than anything else in the world. I can promise you that for an infant, a breast half full of milk is more vital for its spiritual and physical growth than anything else.

Also, from early on, we are taught the power of resilience. In some countries, by now resilience has grown into equal terms with patriotism. We swim with the masses or go under. But we also start carrying resentment, lies, falseness, and even fakery and then wonder why we are getting lost in all of it. We are lost—and with that, our self-value and self-respect are lost. More and more, we are getting prepared to value and respect everything and everybody but ourselves, because the "should"s of a pluralistic economic society demand us to do so. After all, we do want to at least be appreciated and seen somehow.

In due course, we learn that despite the fact that we have duly responded to all "should"s—we even could have experienced respect for our looks, abilities, or role at that very specific moment in time on the odd occasion in the process—we just cannot gain self-respect from others. And again, the latter causes stress, and stress is toxic.

Self-respect comes from within—from that half-full glass that Mum gave me and from the unconditional loving embrace I received when I was a newborn. Sadly, the coach towards self-respect has left us; it's gone. What can we do now? By now we have become aware of the fact that on our search for authenticity, people come our way who actually detect our lack of self-respect and self-care. We may even have been told that we put others before ourselves—and to a great extent, such as giving beloved belongings away, depriving ourselves of simple treasures.

Lack of self-respect does, indeed, include the essence of self-care. We have lost the value of giving ourselves rest, relaxation, and pleasure, because the "should" list has become very long and even more demanding. In short, with the loss of our self-love, self-value, and self-respect we also have lost our own truth. We also could have lost that very truth right in the beginning of our existence when we did not receive the unconditional embrace from Mum—when she hugged her little dream girl whilst holding her baby son. We lost that very truth when we did not receive the unconditional embrace from Dad when he hugged the little boy of whom he was so proud whilst Mum's energy might have flown through as mere negative disappointment that her husband was not able to give her a little, wee girl.

With coming into this world as a certain gender—girl or boy—we already have taken our first step into a pluralistic, economy-driven society full of values and future aims in which the value of the here and now—the day of your very birth—became neglected. If mum and dad wanted a girl and you came as a girl, you were lucky. At least you received the public confidence of being a girl. If you, however, arrived as a boy—boy, I'd feel sorry for you. You will have missed out on that public confidence; you also will have missed out on your self-confidence. In the end, it does not matter as what gender we enter this world. We are *who* we are, girl or boy. We are a continuance of the greater existence.

As a girl or a boy, you will also have made your acquaintance with the value of being the gender you have come into this world with. You will have noticed that your male siblings were treated differently compared with your female siblings. You are learning how to be an accepted girl or boy. You will start to live for the ideals, needs, and expectations of others—and down the drain self-respect goes once again. Your own needs became belittled and own opinions humiliated. As a result, you have learnt how not to care for yourself. What's the point? But if you have been somewhat smart—and I believe we all have become very smart as a matter of life and death—you will have learnt the skills of disguise. You have become well trained to offer acts of kindness and services to others. One of the biggest pluralistic society commandments is "Love thy neighbor!"

Also, the rest of the pluralistic economic society commandments will be acted out skilfully. You will have learnt to pay extreme attention to how you should look. You will have skilfully adapted to the need for a given excessive order and control in your environment. Your own comfort and relaxation are not important. What is important is that you fit in with the conformism of comfort and relaxation. You have added another role onto your multiple role-plays; you have become a conformist. This role, though, is overriding any other role you may be allowed to play. In a lot of ways, we have learnt to project out what we do not do for ourselves. That way, the authority of a pluralistic society can read you very well and can keep control over you.

At this point, I like to draw attention once again to one of my favourite philosophers, Kahlil Gibran. He was a Lebanese-American artist, poet, and writer. His book, *The Prophet,* was a 1923 inspirational fiction work with a series of philosophical essays written in poetic English prose. It sold very well, despite an initial cool and critical reception. It became extremely popular in the world's 1960s culture in which a trend of renaissance was felt like an outcry for more than the society of the time obviously could offer to its population. Gibran has become the third-best-selling poet of all time, following Shakespeare and Lao-Tzu. In his book, *The Prophet,* Gibran writes of children:

> *Your children are not your children.*
> *They are the sons and daughters of Life's longing for itself.*
> *They come through you but not from you,*
> *And though they are with you, yet they belong not to you.*

You may give them your love but not your thoughts.
For they have their own thoughts.
You may house their bodies but not their souls,
For their souls dwell in the house of tomorrow,
which you cannot visit, not even in your dreams.
You may strive to be like them, but seek not to make them like you.
For life goes not backward nor tarries with yesterday.
You are the bows from which your children as living arrows are sent forth.
The archer sees the mark upon the path of the infinite,
and He bends you with His might
that His arrows may go swift and far.
Let your bending in the archer's hand be for gladness;
For even as he loves the arrow that flies,
so He loves also the bow that is stable. [3]

When I read this poem, I was a sole mother of a then four-year-old girl. The journey towards my own more authentic existence began. In that poem, I realized the importance, relevance, and essence of being a parent. I already had noticed my daughter's longing for "its" own life. I learnt to accept that, yes, I had given birth to her, but also that she came through me, not from me. Each day she was with me, I had to accept—despite the society I lived in—that my little daughter did not belong to me. I started to give her more love and fewer thoughts. Instead, I listened to her thoughts more and more. Eventually I realized the value of housing her body and could accept that I was unable to house her soul. As a matter of fact, I started disliking the thought of housing her soul. Our house would have become a prison for her.

My little girl's soul dwelled in the house of tomorrow, and eventually I could even witness this. This was a very enlightening experience, I admit. I did strive to be like her and learnt a lot from my daughter. When I—and I admit that I did at times—tried to make her like me, it naturally failed. Yes, I was in touch with the pain that went through my body, and I accepted this as a letting-go pain. My little daughter was growing up steadily, and the pain scale within me told me when that happened. It also became obvious to me that life was not going backwards. All the lessons from my past about parenting my daughter did not belong into her life. The past was past; today is today. I imagined becoming the bow from which my daughter—a living arrow—was sent forth. To me, that was the beginning of respect. I had a strong inner connection to these bows and started to *respecere* (to look at) them. And with this, I learnt to see the mark upon the path of the infinite—the unknown. This process gave me the strength to see how I was bent with creation's infinite might. I could, after all, remember that I was initially also part of this creation—lucky me. From then on, I left behind fears and panic over what might become of my daughter. The archer's arrows would go swift and far, I was sure. In that poem, self-love and self-respect came to me. And I never will forget the day this happened.

As you read through this chapter, you may think, *Oh well; we are lost, then, in the values of a pluralistic, economy-driven society and don't have a clue what self-respect and self-value are any longer. So what?* Carl Jung, a Swiss psychiatrist, influential thinker, and founder of analytical psychology once said, "Until you make the unconscious conscious, it will direct your life and you will call it fate." It was *The Prophet* that had directed my life back towards individuality. I did not call it fate back then; I remember calling it luck.

Television is nowadays our most precious technological belonging. In this, I would like to acknowledge the power of media and broadcasting. For instance, CNN, the US cable news channel founded in 1980 by Ted Turner, was the first channel to provide twenty-four-hour television news coverage and the first all-news television channel in the US. As of August, 2010, CNN became available in over 100 million US households. Broadcast coverage extends now to over 890,000 American hotel rooms, and the US broadcast is shown in Canada. Globally, CNN programming airs through CNN International, which can be seen by viewers in over 212 countries and territories. Starting in late 2010, the domestic version of CNN/US became available in high definition to viewers in Japan under the name of CNN HD.

In mid/late October, 2011, I noticed a program on CNN aired under the title *Your Money*. CNN promotes this show with the following words: "They are the biggest issues in your life: your job, your savings, your home, and your debt. *Your Money* breaks down the business news of the week and shows you how it impacts your bottom line." Now, listen to this message our young generation is receiving carefully. When we think about the initially mentioned value and origin of belonging, it becomes obvious how far we have moved away from *being and* reaching. We seem to only reach.

It is never too late for anybody—no matter what culture, beliefs, or age—to examine his or her balance of being and reaching by asking some of the following questions: Do I respect my values, opinions, self-care, actions, intentions, and motivations? What is, in fact, the meaning of respect in terms of my own self, including the family into which I was born? These are questions worth looking at. They are crying out for answers. Any answer you will be able to give will be a new start towards self-respect and self-value. You will, consequently, nearly automatically make adjustments to a more authentic you.

> He removes the greatest ornament of friendship,
> who takes away from it respect.
>
> **Cicero (106-43 BC)**

RESPECT TOWARDS FRIENDS

Ayn Rand, a Russian-American novelist and philosopher who only just died twenty years ago, said, "If one doesn't respect oneself one can have neither love nor respect for others." [4] This chapter leads our newborn to his or her first steps into kindergarten and later into school and university. Friendships will start to be built, and some may last for years to come; some may only last for weeks.

Depending how your child will have perceived your respect, he or she will hopefully have gained both a positive feeling of esteem for a person, religion, nation, or specific behaviour or action and a specific conduct representing this esteem. Within the society your child is growing up in, specific ethics of respect will be taught and so will specifics of disrespect. A certain conduct in one country might be considered a polite one but can well be considered a rude one in another country. Culture has got a mighty say in regard to how we denote respect. But for the time being, your child is only learning your home culture.

Through modern technology, though—TV, Internet, etc.—new cultures may visit us on a daily basis right in our living rooms. Your child will pick up whatever is foreign to her or him. How you as a parent are dealing with this foreignness will be a teaching tool towards whether your child respects foreignness or not. The same applies to any friends your girl or boy will bring home. They might be from a different country, have a different status in society, or believe in a different religion than you do. Your child's perception of this foreignness still very much depends on how you will react to foreignness as a parent.

Respect, though, should not be confused with tolerance. Tolerance does not imply any positive feelings as such. Remember your newborn; your feelings towards the world and positive attitude are the road to respect, and this road is infinitively long. Specific ethics of respect are fundamentally important to various cultures. Respect for tradition and legitimate authority is one fundamental moral value shared by different societies and individuals. Any disapproval from your side will be picked up by your child. Disrespect is learnt. It is that simple.

Also be aware that respect is shown in many languages by specific grammatical conventions, especially in referring to individuals. Language is a powerful tool, and your *lingua* comes with your culture. You may refer to a neighbour as "this horrible man" rather than "Mr. Smith," and your child will pick this up. Or you may talk of another neighbour who you are very fond of and refer to as "this truly humble woman." Again, your child will pick this judgement up. As a parent, you are the road-builder towards respect or disrespect in your child. The fewer judgements you use, the better.

Needless to say, there are outside road-builders towards respect in form or positions, which I call roles. The first role your child comes in touch with is you, the mother, simply by birth. Later roles will be the father, a brother, a sister, grandmother and grandfather, a teacher, priest, politician, lawyer, doctor—in short everybody who is publicly, legally, or in any other official way in charge. Again, these roles are respected differently in different countries or cultures, and your child will pick up respect or disrespect towards them through the eye of the public, be it radio, television, Internet, etc.

Probably the least-recognized forms of the road towards respect are the much-unspoken ones—your gestures and manners. Children will pick these up the easiest, as they do not have any confusing explanations attached to them.

Gestures are simple and clear. For instance, in the western European and American culture, raising your arm to greet a person is a sign of respect to let the other person see that he or she has been recognized. Not purposely recognizing somebody you know can be the most awful sign of disrespect and could attract a deep sensation of rejection in the person not feeling recognized.

Now, your child will have gathered everything important for himself or herself on the road towards respect and choose his or her friends accordingly. Your child will know by school-entry that people around him or her can be the objects or recipients of various forms of respect. Your daughter or son will have seen his or her father respecting another person's legal rights or will have noticed how the Americans respect their president by calling him "Mr. President." Your son will have noted a healthy respect in his father for an easily angered person or will have seen his mother respecting someone by caring for this person. As a parent, you will have cherished your child in his or her solid particularity, which often will be expressed as a gentle sigh of respect. And as long as this sigh is gentle, it will come across as respectful.

If you as a parent respect an individual for his or her commitment to a worthy project and accord one person the same basic moral respect any person deserves, you will have built a very solid road towards the ability to respect within your child.

Yet in the child's eye, the idea of respect for people still can be somewhat ambiguous, as both institutional respect and evaluative respect can be for persons in roles or positions. Sometimes it might not be transparent for your child as to why a certain or specific person has been respected by you. Was it because the person was your teacher, and simply because of that, your mother respected her or him, or was it because the person deserved your mother's attention because your mother felt the need to care for this very person?

Your child will have the right to choose his or her own preferences of respect. It is up to you as a parent to let your child have this particular right. Ethically and philosophically, the notion of respect for people in general means a kind of respect that all people are owed morally just because they are persons, regardless of social position, roles, individuality, character traits, achievements, or moral merit.

Your child, though, along with his or her newfound friends, will now also learn of respect in ways that may be constrained by certain sacred limits. This might come to them in terms of rights. The fundamental right to respect simply because they are persons will be challenged to extreme limits. We all are learning through life the difference between respecting a person for who she or he *is* and respecting a person for what she or he *does*. It depends on the moral standards of your society which actions of a person can be respected and which cannot. You know the saying: "Actions speak louder than words."

But children initially are still able to simply pick up the energy that is carried with any action or word. Intuition and gut feelings are still very active in young children. Whereas it might have been commonplace for your child that people are owed or have a right to equal respect, it is also obvious that certain actions of people cannot owe every individual evaluative respect, let alone equal evaluative respect. Remember, not everyone acts morally or correctly or even possesses an equally moral, good character. Your child will, consequently, learn a concept for his or her assessment, in which respect for a person has to be analysed as some form of recognition or reverential respect. And again, it is in this context that your child will seek preferences in characteristics or actions in his or her environment and choose friends towards these preferences. Make the best of it, parents, because your definition and practice of respect will be challenged, too.

> That you may retain your self-respect, it is
> better to displease the people by doing what
> you know is right, than to temporarily please
> them by doing what you know is wrong.
>
> **William J. H. Boetcker**

RESPECT TOWARDS AUTHORITIES

Continuing on his or her live journey, your child will soon make contacts with so-called authorities. The first authority figure that I was told to respect as my duty was any teacher who came my way during school years. For my mother, a teacher was *the* authority of all; later followed doctors, ministers, and business relations in our environment. The larger the cycle of authorities that I had to respect grew, the larger my curiosity about what respect essentially meant grew. I got as confused as your child would have become by now when we finished the second chapter, "Respect Towards Friends."

I like to take a little time at this stage to look at what defines authority in our world. A person who has the power or right to control, judge, or prohibit the actions of others according to universal public definitions is an authority figure. Hence, in the small eyes of a child, *anybody* who is a grown-up is an authority. A group with this power, such as a government, police force, military, etc. will also be an authority—specifically, obviously, those who wear any kind of uniform. Within this context, there are roles which automatically are owed respect to as an authority—all those who are in authority. These persons are automatically authorities in the line of duty.

Then there are the so-called experts who can be authorities; they have mainly earned their respect by doing what they are doing. The word *authority,* while we're on the subject, was derived from the Latin *auctōritas* and from the French *autorité.* Its Latin origin simply means "the power to determine, adjudicate, or otherwise settle issues or disputes." It also includes the right to control, command, or determine. Hence it becomes more and more obvious that a child learns the value of respect through honouring people for what they do or who they are in the public eye but not for who they are as individual people.

If the loving eye within your "I—thou" relationship in the early beginnings of your child has been a weak one and the energy of unconditional love for your child has not flown freely, your child by now will be very mixed up with who to respect or who not to respect. By now, for your child, the value of respect has become a demand—"You *must* respect!"

This can lead to a very detrimental result. But let's remember John Gray. Gray was born in 1948 and became a British political philosopher who viewed humanity as a ravenous species engaged in wiping out other forms of life. He was the one who said, "Humans cannot destroy the Earth, but they can easily wreck the environment that sustains them." And, yes, he started out as a child, too, and learnt a principle lesson on his road to respect. He said, "When men and women are able to respect and accept their differences then love has a chance to blossom." [5] John Gray must have received this unconditional energy flow in the "I—thou" relationship with his first contact with a human being. Despite his learning of a very destructive environment, he still knew of the essence of love.

Coming back to my childhood—I have to admit that over the years, I have lost a lot of respect for any kind of authority unless a person in charge showed integrity. And it is integrity that I respect the most. Integrity, for me, is the most important essence to accept in any person, be it in an authority figure, parent, or whatever. I have not met John Gray personally but assume that he was one of the few authors who lived his life according to his teachings. There are a lot of teachers, authors, and authorities out there who do not live what they teach. To me, that shows a lack of integrity. When a person does not integrate various parts of his or her personality into a harmonious, intact whole—which in my view, includes his or her profession or trade—this person, in my understanding, disobeys moral and ethical principles, soundness, moral character, and honesty and becomes unworthy of respect.

From my school days, I specifically remember my mathematics teacher, who also taught the subjects of physics and chemistry. This teacher was attending to his students in a very unique way; he was different from other teachers of different subjects. My math teacher gave me respect and attention, even when I was weak at a given task, and always was very eager to help and to turn that weakness into strength. I became a good math student, and the subjects of physics and chemistry came easily to me because of this very present teacher. On the contrary, I had a geography teacher who also taught biology. In both subjects, I failed early on, as my subject teacher was judgemental and disrespectful—not only to me, but also to other classmates when they showed weakness in understanding his subjects.

From that, I learnt that respect is the first positive step in building a relationship. I learnt not only to respect the math teacher but also the subjects of his teachings, whereas initially I had problems respecting the geography teacher and his subjects. Only later, when I learnt of the importance of wholeness and integration, did I look again at geography and biology and learnt to love these subjects as well. I could detach these subjects from a person who did not deserve my respect.

Relationships—no matter with whom or what—are central to conflict transformation. Also, goals are easier to attain when the element of respect is present. I would like to go as far as to say that if you want to come across as a human being, you cannot be arrogant (like my geography teacher was).

Yes, I agree that every human being and nation, irrespective of power or strength, deserves to be respected. Being respected means being treated with consideration and esteem; respect means being willing to treat people similarly. Let's remember that respect is the opposite of humiliation and contempt. Where the latter can be a cause of conflict, the former and its opposite can help transform it. I would like to quote William Ury here, who wrote in his book, *The Third Side,* "Human beings have a host of emotional needs—for love and recognition, for belonging and identity, for purpose and meaning to live. If all these needs had to be subsumed in one word, it might be respect." [6] William Ury is the co-founder of Harvard's Program on Negotiation and is at present a Senior Fellow of the Harvard Negotiation Project.

As my different authority figures from the past—the math teacher and the geography teacher—have taught me, respect indeed allows one to build trust or distrust with the other. But furthermore, respect also allows me to build and rebuild relationships, because it provides me with a neat gateway into the other side of a person or a subject. The neatness refers to the presence of respect, which can lead to a positive change, whilst its nonexistence would lead to even more destruction. This unique gateway will create opportunities. I would say that it is vital as a parent to show this gateway to your children. When you treat your children with respect, you as the first authority are able to show them respect from different angles.

In any conflict, treat the other person with civility and honour. You don't need to jump to the same level the other person is coming from. The first rule of paying respect is to stay in your respectful level. Any person who is being given respect will be more willing to make compromises. With that in mind, solutions are doable.

Even in dealing with authorities, we have to remind our children of the biblical quotation: "Do unto others as you would others do unto you." The secret is to treat others as you want to be treated. As a child has unconditional love in the "I—thou" relationship with his or her mother in the first days of life, so does respect grow by nourishing itself from its own process and dynamics. Always be the first to respect. With time, this will develop amongst all conflicting parties, be they parents, friends, authority figures, or even subjects. Keep being courteous towards your children and what they have to say. Treat them fairly to maintain an atmosphere of trust—in other words, respect. They are your children, and you are their authority. Your children are digging into an important treasure chest in everyday life. You taught them to be respected and to respect their teachers, the elderly, school rules, traffic laws, family traditions, cultural traditions, other people's feelings, your country's leaders, the truth, and even people's differing opinions.

Then one day, you will witness your near grown-up child shaking his or her head at people who seem not to have learnt to respect them, as I witnessed with the geography teacher. Your child will start to respect only those who are, in his or her perception, truly worthy of his or her respect. At least I came to the conclusion in my early school years that to some degree, not everybody automatically justifies my personal approach of respect. I learnt about boundaries and added those to my treasure chest in which also the aim was put that nevertheless, all people are worthy of respect.

I learnt over time that jobs and relationships would become unbearable if I received no respect in them. In certain milieus, your child may learn the price of disrespect if he or she violates the street law: "Diss me, and you die."

Respect towards authority is neither owed nor earned, per se, in my understanding. There is a vice-versa conduct involved which either gives way to respect or disrespect. Respect is a matter of how we relate to each other. We have to, of course, see our political and community sets of rules as a different subject of respect altogether. Needless to say, calls to respect this or that are increasingly part of public life in today's critical world. Certain groups of environmentalists call on respect for nature. Other groups in your community disrespect the thought and act of abortion. Capital punishment representatives call for respect for human beings. Such demands for respect nevertheless are best served when these demands take place under terms of mutual respect.

By the time your child has grown up and is off to his or her first job or professional duties, he or she will have fully integrated his or her individual concept of respect. Your child will have noticed how respect in general is understood or even what category of thing respect is in itself. Your son or daughter will have noticed the complexity of difference in how respect will be expressed, be it as a mode of behaviour, form of treatment, kind of valuating, type of attention, motive, attitude, feeling, tribute, principle, duty, entitlement, moral virtue, or epistemic virtue and will have asked herself or himself if any of these forms of respect could be more central to his or her understanding than others.

With this is mind, we approach the next chapter, "Respect Towards Colleagues."

> Respect a man; he will do the more.
>
> **James Howell**

RESPECT TOWARDS COLLEAGUES

The working environment of your now grown-up child will confront her or him with many questions regarding the essence of respect all over again. We have learnt that all our lives go much better when we respect the things that deserve to be respected. We also can respect some things independently of considerations of how our lives would go.

But at the time we come into contact with our colleagues, we are meeting such a diversity of people that effectively, more questions about respect will arise. One of the many questions would be what beliefs, attitudes, emotions, motives, and last but not least, what conduct respect involves and what respect is incompatible with in a new environment full of new people now called colleagues.

After a dispute with one of your colleagues about a certain task in your job, you may come to ask yourself, *What are the appropriate objects of respect (i.e., the sorts of things that can be reasonably said to warrant respect in this specific case)?* What is, in fact, the basis of respect—the features or facts about objects in virtue which it is reasonable and perhaps obligatory to respect? You may ask yourself, *What moral requirements, if any at all, are there to respect this colleague's unwavering attitude in this specific task, and what would be my approach to avoid disrespect?*

Your child might feel his or her own virtue to respect but be unable to agree on the attitude of this colleague's towards the task. Your child might also fear that this conflict might substantially harm the outcome of the task to which he or she holds more respect than this specific colleague. This conflict leads to the overall question of what the implications of respect for problematic issues are in the first place. Your child will come across a multiple array of problems; that is for sure.

We only have to look at socio-political issues—racism, sexism, pornography, privacy, punishment, responses to terrorism, paternalism in health care contexts, cultural diversity, affirmative action, abortion and so it goes on. In today's life, everything comes as a problem, per se, doesn't it? Despite the widespread acknowledgement of the importance of respect in moral and political life and theory, your grown-up child will find that there is, in fact, no settled agreement in either everyday thinking or philosophical discussion about such issues as how to understand the concepts, what the appropriate objects of respect are, what is involved in respecting objects, what the conditions for self-respect are, and so on.

In the environment of work, we come along a vast diversity of human qualities as well as an equally vast diversity of significance of work in itself—and with it, the quintessence of respect may become even more confusing. There are as many meanings to respect as there are people and objects.

We have to look back once more to our "I—thou" relationship that started our life in the honouring arms of our first present parent, through whom we perceived and hopefully received the energy of unconditional love. We then can *"respicere"* or look back at our personal value of love—

self-love. I find this way of primal teaching of respect the most valuable. The greatest value of things in general can be found in their simplicity.

We have by now met a lot of people and could detect that many lives depend very much on whether a person respects herself or himself or not. Unfortunately, we cannot take the value of self-respect for granted. But any one of us will have discovered at some stage of his or her life how very important it is when self-respect seems threatened, finding that we haven't got it in the first place or may have lost it somewhere in the jungle of life. In working with colleagues, these findings will be the most vital of any learning of being employed. Being employed and working for an authority figure, for an object, and alongside colleagues presents itself with numerous chores of exercising respect. Some of us who will be in the unfortunate situation to find that self-respect has been lost will need to regain it. Others, who have not completely lost self-respect as such, find themselves struggling to develop or maintain it while having to work in a hostile environment.

At this point, I recall a situation when I was employed and had to work for a very lovely boss who treasured the value of my work very much. I knew I was good at my job and received lots of positive responses for doing what I was doing. Though I was good at my job, that did not at all mean that I had much self-respect. I knew by the time I was in the workforce that I needed to compensate self-respect through work. I was intelligent, flexible, and could coordinate certain tasks to perfection. I knew this, and for that I respected myself. But I was not at the point yet where I could adamantly say, "I respect myself."

My "I—thou" primary source of experiencing unconditional love had been very early destroyed due to the socio-political situation of the country I was living in. I was picked up into a hard-working environment of the post-WWII years where work and reward for a good work done brought my country strong values of esteem. In the role of a worker, I was good. I had earned respect for my role but had lost self-respect somewhere on the

33

way. One day at work, one of my colleagues made his dislike of me working alongside him in the company very much known. I had originally always figured that this colleague was threatened by my perfectionism in my work and feared he would lose his as a consequence. But this stayed unspoken to the day. He initiated a fight which ended up with me running back into my office, crying. The pain of being disrespected and more or less bullied was very strong, as I remember. I had to step my mind away from this pain and rescue myself by going into my rational space—my head—to figure out what actually had happened. In that process, I realized that my colleague's initiation of this very fight was only for one reason—to get me out of his sight. Well, I was not ready to resign just for a person like that. I went back into his office and said in very calm words what I thought of him and that his opinion of me ultimately would mean nothing to me.

I still remember his wide-open eyes and a slow, emerging smile on his face. I was puzzled. I knew instantly he was not laughing at me, but what did his smile mean? He sat there for a while, looking at me and smiling, and I stood in front of him for a while, wondering what next needed to happen. Then he stood up. His smile changed into loud laughter, and while he was giving me a bigger-than-big hug, he shouted out loud, "I knew, girl, you had it in you. You can actually stand up for yourself. Well done!"

And I had learnt my lesson. I was finally able to respect myself alongside this colleague. I had regained my self-respect. In the years to come, I still would be challenged by male colleagues until I found the reason why I seemed to lose my self-respect when having to deal with men. They stood for the authoritative father figure, which I never had. I never met my father through all my life. He had been taken away from me during the war years and was, just like me, a victim of WWII.

Sadly, during the process of such disillusioned experiences, some people will discover that their life is no longer worth living. Self-respect has become irretrievable.

In the late 1990s, New Zealand was recognized as having the worst suicide rates in the world for youth aged fifteen to twenty-four. Indicators showed that youth suicide rates of this age group have declined since then, but still, the suicide rate in New Zealand's youth between fifteen and nineteen remains alarmingly high compared with other countries. Suicides are a marker not just of individuals who are unable to overcome a challenge or crisis for whatever reason, but also of unaddressed mental disorders and drug and alcohol abuse—in short, of a lack of social cohesion and integration.

People may commit suicide because they realize their lack of skills or resilience to overcome problematic issues when they encounter them. They find themselves inadequate of necessary factors to avoid a suicide.

Two certain necessary factors to avoid suicide are self-respect and lack of respect being paid. It is part of everyday wisdom that respect and self-respect are deeply interconnected. In my opinion, it is difficult—if not impossible—both to respect others if we don't respect ourselves and to respect ourselves if others don't respect us. It is becoming more and more known that unreasonable social institutions can damage self-respect incredibly. On the other hand, a genial and resilient self-respect can be a potent force in struggles against injustice.

Of course, there are different kinds of respect—as we already have touched on—and these differences complicate the matter of the essence of respect highly. One general distinction is between respect simply as a behaviour and respect as an attitude or feeling, which may or may not be expressed in or signified by behaviour. To understand this, we only have to look at my given example with my colleague, who had started to treat me without respect for the only reason that I did not know how to respect him as a man. A person who respects somebody or something pays attention to that person or to that something. Let's be reminded of the word *respecere*. When we are able to look at somebody or something, we are able to respect. When we are able to look at ourselves, we are capable of self-respect.

In this context, it is vital to recognize the art of perception. We all perceive differently. That makes us unique. My personal encounter with my colleague back then clearly showed the unique perception of each part in this very encounter. My colleague saw my weak self-respect at that time, and I perceived this man from a lack of being able to *respicere*—to look back at a man due to the lack of a male role model in my upbringing. If it wouldn't have been for my work respect with which I compensated my lack of self-respect, I could have no doubt ended up in dire desperation.

In a work situation, you will be very much challenged to see the objects of your respect clearly as they really are in their own right and not seeing them solely through the filter of your own desires, fears, likes, or dislikes. Calling in my work respect was consequently the result of re-birthing my self-respect. In other words, though my "I—thou" primary source of experiencing unconditional love had been very early destroyed due to the socio-political situation of the country I was living in, it was in its essence not destroyed.

I have lived and worked in Germany, Spain, and the United States over the years and have worked the last twenty years in New Zealand. No other country besides New Zealand has shown me this incredible new lifestyle of bringing work home. It didn't matter if I worked in Germany, Spain, or the USA; work was work, and leisure time was leisure time. Respect was given where and whenever it was due.

Then again, Germany, Spain, and the USA—at least during the years before the big recession phenomena hit the world—offered a wide range of leisure time activities. These countries do, in fact, pride themselves on having a leisure time industry. Such industry does not exist in New Zealand due to reasons I don't want to explore further in this context. And if it exists, it only aims for tourists and feeds the tourism industry—a rather anonymous target for respect in a pluralistic economic society, I'd say.

I am more concerned about the fact that the individual might not be able any longer to separate itself from the obligation to work and the obligation to cherish a family. In what kind of dynamic and energy are our New Zealand children growing up? Will work and earning money be more valued, more respected than your own family? Is the need for money already eliminating all values of cherishing a family? Will our colleagues become mere competitors for a common goal in a pluralistic economic society? Or shouldn't we pay our respect to our family through work? Shouldn't we respect our children more than our bank balance sheet? Shouldn't our colleagues become the target of our respect in order to serve our common goal of being able to support and respect all of our families? I think these questions are worth thinking about.

Some people have so much respect for their superiors they have none left for themselves.

Peter McArthur

RESPECT TOWARDS PROPERTY AND ASSETS

When we come home from work, we are with our families or on our own. We are not surrounded by colleagues and bosses or any other types of authorities; we are in our homes, surrounded by our furniture and belongings. We could classify these as our assets.

In this environment, another aspect of respect will need to be looked at: the care respect. We see this aspect of respect mostly exemplified in the environmentalist's deep desire for the respect for nature. Care respect regards an object as having a profound and even unique value. The energy of unconditional love of our first parent that made its way into our heart is as strong as the environmentalist's desires to cherish his or her natural environment. The care respect shares, in fact, deep roots with self-respect.

Some people may look at the care respect from a feminist ethic of care. In my eyes, that has nothing to do with feminist ethics. I assume that such understanding may have its roots in the cultural separation process from matriarch into patriarch. But we must not forget that we all are born into this life by our mothers; no matriarch or patriarch can deny that. As such, we all will have a way to *respicere*—to look back at the first process of our life during which we either did or did not perceive the flow of unconditional love coming through to us.

Let's again reflect back on Martin Buber's suggestion that we may address existence in two ways, the first being the "I" towards an "it" existence and the second being the "I" towards "thou" existence. The first existence is towards an object as a separate self, and the second is moving into existence in a relationship without bounds. Meaningfulness, Buber had stated, is found in human life in relationships, and all of our relationships ultimately bring us to God, the eternal thou.

You will ask yourself, *Where is this leading? What do my assets or property have to do with an eternal thou, let alone with respect?* Care respect reflects much on how much we care for our property or assets, furniture, and belongings. Again, there are many ways to respect these. We can keep our distance from them by escaping the seeming emptiness of our home. We can destroy them willingly or by chance; we can protect them or be careful around them. We can talk about them when we are with friends or colleagues to evaluate their worth or status. We can mourn about a loss of them, or we can nurture them by keeping them clean and in order.

Look at a teenager, for instance, who disdains adults for the sake of using an object. He or she will behave respectfully towards a friend's parent in order to get the car. In reality, this teenager was in fact disrespectful, because his or her outwardly respect towards the friend's parent with the aim to get the car was purely an act of manipulation. Any kind of manipulation disregards the essence of respect. This example also makes the use of respect—the seemingly outwardly and respectful approach towards the friend's parent—visible and adds another dimension to the confusion of the meaning of respect altogether. If the car would have been stolen from the garage, it would have been a clear sign of disrespect. But we have been brainwashed into respecting. The demand only to respect others does ultimately not give a person the fundamental nature of respect. We have learnt to use means of respect in order to gain something.

As we pay respect by certain means, we simply pay the price for an asset. And when the price is paid, the deal is done. Yet when we simply respect, there is no deal done, as there was no need to enter into a contract. When we respect, we get respect.

The dealings in regard to gaining assets have shifted the balance of paying and getting. Money has started to rule the world. Mind you, there is still the saying, "You get what you pay for." If we look at respect, this saying has got a conclusive meaning. But mostly, this saying refers to a deal in which monetary exchange was involved. Gaining respect doesn't cost anything but your mere action of showing or giving respect. Gaining a desirable object can cost from as little as you can afford to as much you cannot afford.

Unfortunately, a trend has been noticed after the years of WWII. If you own valuable assets, you are thought to be well off, and obviously then you are respected by others. Now see yourself coming home from work and leaving your contacts, colleagues, customers, clients, etc. behind. You are surrounded by your assets. If you are lucky, you live on your own property in a modest or luxury home. This is your place—where you supposedly belong—and you are in the midst of your belongings.

The term "belonging" has shifted as much from its original meaning as the term "respect" has. The term "belong" is a present participle of "be" and "long." Interestingly, the word "long" originates from the Old High German "*bilangen*," which in English translates to "to reach." In other words, "I am" and "I reach" build a connection. If I visualize this connection, I can see the baby being (it is too little to be able to do anything) and reaching instinctively for "being" fed—that is, reaching for the food source of the mother's breast milk and for her closeness at the same time. If the breastfeeding process happens from this very stage of being on both parts—mother being and feeding, the baby being and reaching—then a mutual formation of belonging is achieved. As this process happens, I like to make the connection with respect with *respicere* (respectively, *respecere*), *looking back at or looking at what both mother and child have experienced in that very moment of first contact being established. We start to recognize our be-longing and continue to nourish this as we have gained the ability of looking back or looking at this very process.*

Just imagine now if this very process had been interrupted for whatever reason or could not get started in the first place. We only would have a mere moment to look back at; in the worst scenario, we would have had not a chance at all to know the meaning of *respicere*. Nor would we have been able to learn the formation of belonging.

The term "belonging" over the years has shifted to various other socially acceptable meanings, from "being part of," "being connected with," "being annexed," or "related to" to "owing allegiance or service" to something or somebody or, last but not least, "being rightly placed in a specified position."

I have always liked the possibility of exploring the meaning and the origin of a word and have found that many origins have gotten lost, as cultures and societies are ever-changing. In the transition of change, a manifold set of confusion enters our life. The origin of "respect" has gone astray; so has the origin of "belonging."

Again, I like to reflect on my own experience in the context of direct care respect—respectively, belonging. As I had mentioned before in the situation with my colleague, I knew myself and respected myself because of my work respect, whereas self-respect was pretty much weakened back then. I had lost it during the very early forced separation from my mother during breastfeeding times. Then I was orphaned and had little contact and no sense of belonging over the next two and a half years until I got fostered and later adopted. All this was due to political and social circumstances. My new mother, having being part of the culture of Emperor Wilhelm during her childhood years and later part of two wars and the magnificent economic miracle years of post-WWII Germany, taught me in a weekly lesson: *"Spare, lerne, leiste was, dann hast du, kannst du, bist du was!"* In English, this means: "Save, learn, achieve something; then you'll have, can, and be something (somebody)." To the day, I don't know where this saying originated from, but I heard it at least once a week. This was the foundation of my new adopted belonging. I learnt to respect saving, learning, and achieving. But I did not learn how to care and knew little about self-respect. Yet I can—with glee, pride, and joy—admit that I never lost the knowledge of yearning for what I had lost.

A post-WWII generation was longing for personal and financial safety as well as for knowledge and information, all of which a Hitler regime had not made possible. And this generation wanted all of this for its children. Self-respect, self-confidence, and self-esteem were not things that were on the priority list of learning. In one way or another, these had shifted towards having them; in other words, a new generation was taught that if you had enough money, knowledge, and assets, consequently, respect, confidence, and esteem would automatically come along for the ride as long as they could show their values on a bank statement. However, this attitude in a consumer-driven society continued into today's societies— into the second and even third post-WWII generations—as the financial global collapse in 2011 has proved. America's downfall in 2011 from being the first in the row of respect, confidence, and esteem has triggered a lethal avalanche, and it took other countries on this ride with it. And it's only now that a realization is kicking in: "Money can't buy happiness," as a *Forbes* article recently bluntly put it.

During my childhood years, I learnt to look at—that is, to *respecere*— appearances. My new mother owned a fashion retail shop, and needless to say, everything from morning through to the evening hours was about appearance. Appearances were another factor of a changing time after WWII. With financial gain, people could dress up and show their social status through their appearance. Emperor Wilhelm and his social class separation between royalists and commoners had shifted towards a social class division of upper, middle, and lower classes. My adopted mother came from the lower class, and by the age of twenty-five, she had entered the middle class by means of saving, learning, and working, respectively. When I came in contact with her, she was busy trying to reach the upper class.

A transition towards the upper class happened when you brought a servant into your home. Due to rules and regulations of adoption requirements, my mother was told she would need a female servant in her home so that the new adopted child—me—could have a twenty-four/seven contact person, as my new mother was busy trying to reach the upper class by working in her retail shop as a successful retailer. The "only the best for the child" rule within adoption requirements further helped my mother achieve this.

With a servant in the house, we appeared to be on a ladder of satisfying success within our community and society. And in 1963, Ludwig Erhard came along. I remember his efforts as a staunch believer of economic liberalism very well. Initially, after the war, Erhard became the economic consultant for the American military administration of Bavaria, which made him Minister of Economics in the Bavarian cabinet of Wilhelm Hoegner. With the American and British administrations crafting the Bizone, Erhard became chairman of the Expert Department for Money and Credit in 1947 and led an expert commission, preparing the necessary currency reform. In this position, Erhard focused upon the general theme of monetary and financial recovery, which affected the adoption of the so-called Homburg Plan in April 1948 that set the stage for the recovery of the economy. On 20 June, 1948, the Deutsche mark was introduced. Erhard abolished the price fixing and production controls that had been enacted by the military administration. Though this step exceeded his authority, he nevertheless succeeded with this courageous step.

During his three years as the German Chancellor, he acted upon his belief that the majority world problems were able to be dissolved through free trade and the economic unity of Europe as a prerequisite for political unification. As young as I was back then, I already realized that economy along with financial trades became the real leaders of politics. And in this, Erhard failed to understand that American global interests, not Europe's political or economic needs, dictated policy in Washington, DC. Erhard had openly rejected Adenauer's policy of fostering good relations with both the US and France in the pursuit of West German national interest.

Specifically, during his last year of reign, I vividly remember Erhard reminding German consumers of the importance of saving versus the obvious spending that went on within the economic miracle years of Germany. He was bluntly laughed at; that I remember equally clearly. When he told people that they needed to save instead of spend, he certainly lost the respect of most who had voted for him. Faced with a dangerous budget deficit in the 1966-1967 recessions, Erhard literally fell from office in part because of concessions that he had made during a visit to President Lyndon B. Johnson.

German families—including the one I belonged to—continued their spending habits, and the journey towards reaching the upper class with values of appearances grew larger and larger. To have became more important than to be.

We now had a profitable, running retail business and a servant who could run the household equally profitably for appearance purposes. But I would not get taught how to maintain assets. All cleaning, washing, and dusting were done by our servant, who was specifically told by my mother that I should in no case get involved in the servant's duties. Hence, I never became a very good housewife, as saving, learning, and achieving had become my most important duties.

When later I left home and had my own home, I realized that whilst saving, learning, and achieving, I could not find time for the maintenance of my home and assets (belongings) to my satisfaction. I realized the importance of care respect. Once my daughter was born, my conflict with care-respect continued. I was running through the day—working, learning, saving, cleaning, and maintaining—because I wanted a lovely-looking environment for my daughter and myself.

When my daughter approached her fourth year, I hosted a St. Claus party at my home. St. Claus came through the door on 6 December, 1982 and sat in my living room with his big bag of presents for the children attending the parties with their mothers. Each child happily received a gift after a little dialogue with St. Claus and then left. The children started happily playing with their new belongings and then heard loud and heavy steps on our entrance stairways. All looked respectfully to the door, as obviously St. Claus was returning to our home, as he might have forgotten something. And indeed, he had. He asked each child to sit on his lap while he said, "Now, look, you have received your gift from St. Claus before, but tell me honestly, what would you really have wished for?"

Loud and clear, my daughter replied in front of all the others, "Well, to be honest, what I really would like to have is a mother who does not do things all the time. I don't want her to be away from me, doing all the time. On Sundays, I want her to be with me, playing and things like that." I was stunned, for the lack of another word. But I also realized the very important difference between having and being.

I also realized that there are many different kinds of objects, assets, or belongings that can reasonably be respected and many different reasons why they deserve respect. Some things warrant respect, as they are dangerous and powerful. Respect of these things can involve fear, awe, self-protection, or submission. For instance, simply all aspects of nature, though beautiful, also can be dangerous and very powerful.

Then again, other things have authority over us. These include acknowledgment of their authority and most likely obedience to their authoritative commands. My mother taught me to be respectful of her and demanded obedience to her authoritative commands.

I could not have spoken to my mother as my daughter did on 6 December in 1982. But looking back at this day, my daughter showed more respect to me by being honest about her needs and towards me as her mother than I could ever have shown to my mother, because I already had been conditioned to be obedient for the sake of freedom in the house and the need for belonging in a family that I had previously lost. My daughter showed to me that I had lost my integrity.

The consequence of the St. Claus event was that I "bought" care respect for my assets, furniture, and need to satisfy appearance; that is, I employed a servant to look after the household needs. I had learnt one lesson; others were to follow. In this lesson, I had learnt to distinguish between two kinds of respect: recognition respect and appraisal respect. Within the first, I had given appropriate weight and consideration to my daughter's respectful (*respicere:* looking back at) and honest deliberation, and within the second, I appraised her for her honest deliberations. Respect is always a two-way approach.

I am now living in New Zealand and am geographically a world apart and some sixty years past the post-WWII phenomena of the economic miracle years. But the call for having and appearance has come into this country as well during the last twenty years. The New Zealand fashion industry is in the process of conquering the world. Twenty years ago, I doubt that the word "fashion" was in fact part of its language dictionary.

Agriculture always has been a major employer and generator of wealth in New Zealand. We also see growth within the manufacturing sectors, with high technology as a cornerstone. With much of the catch exported to Asian markets, the fishing industry—with the Pacific Ocean right in front of our coastline—is also of ever-increasing economic importance.

And, of course, with so much to see, explore, and do, tourism has become a major source of income prior to the American downfall and recession setting in, with travel costs now increasing worldwide. Up to recently, around two million visitors per year have come to travel to New Zealand.

Within New Zealand's natural environment, fast-flowing rivers have been harnessed for the production of electricity. Around 80 percent of power generation is hydroelectric. The rest comes from gas, geothermal, and wind power.

In short, New Zealand has in many ways caught up with the rest of the world; however, this is to the detriment of values of respect whilst its population is more and more becoming a culture of "to have" and leaving its core value of "to be" behind. The crime rate has gone up; so has the use of alcohol and drugs and sadly, family violence. These are signs of the time!

With all these industries in place, even little New Zealand experiences disrespect if it comes to other people's property. Just one example: In August of 2011, a "good Samaritan" couple in the process of helping three men jump start a vehicle were repaid by having their home burgled and their $40,000 car stolen and torched. This good, respectful couple was going out for the evening on a Saturday night when they came across a broken-down car outside their rural home. Of course, they stopped to help. Without success, they tried to jump start the vehicle before continuing on their journey to smell the roses. Upon returning home, they found their car missing. It was later found burnt out. Not only was this kind of senseless crime committed, but also alcohol, cash, a TV, and a camera had been stolen from their home. Yes, the two men who were in charge of such disrespect were found and remanded in custody, accused of burglary and car damage.

This example makes it obvious: disrespect is only a one-way approach.

> The first question I ask myself when something doesn't seem to be beautiful is why do I think it's not beautiful. And very shortly you discover that there is no reason.
>
> **John Cage (1912-1992)**

RESPECT TOWARDS OUR ENVIRONMENT

Though people are the obvious paradigm objects of moral recognition and respect, I believe that they are by far not the only objects we ought to respect with integrity. We have to consider nature, as well, in general—animals, all living creatures, and for that matter, all living things, including viruses and bacteria; the natural ecosystem of our planet; even mountains, rocks, and rivers; and to go beyond our planet, the universe.

Within the aspect of nature, I always prefer to look at the beauty-and-the-beast ambivalence which nature delivers to us; this is very much so during the last years. As much as an iceberg, for instance, will give the observer an admiring, awe-filled response, it can raise in the same person an equally alarming fear response all at the same time when a person observes this wonderful marvel of nature.

As such, nature demands not only moral recognition respect but also authority respect. I agree with the saying that what we owe everything is an opportunity to reveal any value it might have rather than assuming that only persons have the kind of value that morally warrants attention. Nature, in fact, simply by itself is revealing its value on a daily basis. The value I put onto it is the value of existence and coexistence. Existence in itself has an inherent worth and consequently deserves respect.

It is with this consideration that I have come to believe that the inherent worth of existence has faded into the background, and the merit of economic gains has been pushed into the foreground. Consequently, in the process we have lost both self-respect and respect of others, respectively, of our environment. We have become users and consumers of our environment. A wide variety of human practices can be listed, ranging from agriculture and urban development to recreation and energy use to technological and biomedical research. And behind these human practices are very strong industries that make human participation nearly anonymous.

How can life be respected in anonymity? It cannot. Subsequently, no one can be made responsible for anything. Responsibility can be looked at as the ability to respond—response-ability. But when anonymity moves slowly yet strongly into generations and following generations of such pluralistic economic societies, it becomes rather futile to even ask for the ability to respond. Integrity in a net of deception fades away with each step of unrecognized response-ability.

There are a lot of environmentalists out there who claim to protect the environment. Immediately, we come to think of the respective industries that are using our environment for better or for worse. The demand for energy, fuel, gasoline, natural gas, oil, coal, electricity, and geothermal energy is dictating our lives; so does the demand for minerals, silver, and gold within the mining industries. How can we protect our environment with such demands ruling our lives?

President Lyndon B. Johnson said something quite valuable back in 1964 whilst signing the Wilderness Act. He was asking humankind to go an extra mile or two to get physically active and clean up at the same time by participating in community cleanup programs. His words were, "If future generations are to remember us with gratitude rather than contempt . . . we must leave them a glimpse of the world as it was in the beginning, not just after we got through with it."

Canada has become known as a country that is very keen to keep up the need to respect nature or other nonperson targets and is calling its population to think beyond itself to the greater good of the community one is living in and the environment, respectively. Canadians are asked to take pride in both and lead by example. The awareness approach is a good tool to start taking action. Ask yourself, "If everyone did what I'm about to be doing, would this trail or park still be as nice?" A lot of "leave no trace" programs were published to help outdoor enthusiasts reduce their environmental impact when they're enjoying the great outdoors.

China recently has been putting much effort in reducing greenhouse gases and is shifting its industry towards this goal. The call for a balanced environment and respecting our resources has become very strong in China. China is in the process of producing respective means for a world populace to live with and utilize such environmentally benefiting products. But it has not always been like that for China. The environment in the People's Republic of China has traditionally been rather neglected as the country concentrated on its rise as an economic power. Chasing the political gains of economic development, local officials in China often overlooked environmental pollution, worker safety, and all public health problems. And despite a recent interest in an environmental reform, pollution has made cancer the leading cause of death in thirty cities and seventy-eight countries, the Ministry of Health had to admit. [7]

Lead poisoning was one of the most common paediatric health problems in China. A sobering 2006 review made it very clear that one third of Chinese children suffered from elevated blood lead levels, with most lead coming from manufacturing of lead acid batteries for cars and electric bikes. Only 1 percent of the country's 560 million city inhabitants (as of 2007) breathed air deemed safe by the European Union. Chinese industry has scored very poorly in energy efficiency. Chinese steel factories used one fifth more energy per ton than the international average. Cement needs 45 percent more power, and ethylene needs 70 percent more than the average per the Word Bank's assessment. [8]

China still receives pollution from both ends of the supply chain: during the production process and by allowing electronic waste to be recycled and dumped in the country. It is difficult for Chinese people to speak out to denounce environmental pollution and the related health consequences. A well-publicized example of a case when people spoke out involved forty-nine employees at Wintek who were poisoned by n-hexane in the manufacturing of touch screens for Apple products. But in 2011, angry parents rioted in the Zhejiang Haijiu Battery Factory when they were confronted with the fact that their children had received permanent neurological damage from lead poisoning. China has hence become a signatory nation of the Stockholm Convention, a treaty to control and phase out major persistent organic pollutants. A plan for action for 2010 included objectives such as eliminating production, import, and use of the pesticides covered under the convention as well as an accounting system for PC (polychlorinated biphenyls) containing equipment, such as transformers, capacitors, or electric motors. China also plans to establish an inventory of POP-contaminated sites by 2015 along with remediation plans. POPs are persistent organic pollutants, as such organic compounds that are resistant to environmental degradation through chemical, biological, or photolytic processes.

Since May, 2009 the Stockholm Convention also covered polybrominated diphenyl-ethers and perfluorooctanesulfonic acid. Perfluorinated compounds are in general associated with altered thyroid function and decreased sperm count in humans. It is, of course, a big challenge for China to control and eliminate POPs, since they often are cheaper than their alternatives or are unintentionally produced and then simply released into the environment to save on treatment costs. Despite money talking, China has achieved some improvements in environmental protection during the recent years. This, I feel, needs to be respected in an environment that still regards the dollar sign more than the sunrise in the morning. The World Bank has confirmed that China is one of the very few countries in the world that has—or maybe I should say has been made—awakened to the needs of planetary longevity.

China has been rapidly increasing its forest cover and is managing to reduce air and water pollution. I wish we could say that for a lot more countries. With part of a $498 billion (USD) economic stimulus package of November 2008, the Chinese government planned to enhance sewage and rubbish treatment facilities to prevent water pollution, accelerate green belt and natural forest planting programs, and increase energy conservation initiatives and pollution projects. This has been noted as the largest effort in China's history in regard to protecting and respecting not only its environment but also its populace. With a total of $34.6 billion invested in clean technology in 2009 alone, China has become the world's leading investor in renewable energy technologies. It has by now produced more wind turbines and solar panels each year than any other country.

Yes, the time has come; children all over the world need to be told to respect nature and its environment. Upon preparing an outdoor trip, students are asked to plan and prepare for this event. They are asked to know the regulations and special concerns for the area they are going to visit. They are also being informed to prepare for extreme weather, hazards, or emergencies. They are advised to schedule their trip to avoid times of high use. It is also recommended to visit in just small groups (i.e., to split bigger groups into groups of four to six.) They are advised to repackage food to minimize waste. They are also told to use a map or compass to eliminate the use of marking paint, rock cairns, or flagging. Yet sadly, when walking the treasured places of nature, how much litter do we find? Is the voice for leaving no traces not heard within the young generation of a consumer-driven society?

When camping, the best advice is to camp at least seventy metres from lakes and streams and keep the campsites small to leave vegetation to do what it does best. Yet we always find traces of somebody having used a campsite far too close to the lake or a river. Is seventy metres too far to walk?

A basic rule is this: leave what you find. In other words, preserve the past by examining but not touching cultural or historic structures and artefacts. We have eyes to do that—a gift from creation itself. And we need teachers to remind our generation and the ones to come of this very gift.

When I visited Antarctica, it was the ship cruise's responsibility to inform us about the value of leaving what you find. No rocks, plants, or any other natural objects from Antarctica were allowed to be picked up as souvenirs. I have heard the same asked when visiting Little Barrier Island in New Zealand some time ago. In both excursions, everybody respected the leave-what-you-find rule. I noticed, though, that when not specifically asked to do this very logical, respectful requirement, people always tended to pick something up. It is the souvenir hunter that comes out here. Souvenir hunters are mere consumers, and consumers have lost the ability to respond to nature's requirements, so it seems.

A huge risk in today's natural environment is the outbreak of fires. It is obvious that campfires can cause lasting impacts to the backcountry. A lightweight stove would be the recommended tool to cook on, and a candlelight lantern is recommended for light for late afternoon or dinner time. In some areas, we find signs that fires are permitted. But also in those areas, caution is advised, and the use of established fire rings, fire pans, or mound fires are the means of choice. Needless to say, all fires should be kept small. A good trick is to use sticks from the ground that can be broken by hand. It is very important to burn all wood and coals to ash, put out the campfire completely, and scatter the cool ashes.

My partner and I very often use our mobile home and stay at various places New Zealand has to offer. We are always amazed how much evidence of the outbreak of big fires we have come across over the years. The most logical recommendations to avoid a bush fire are lost when not practiced.

I would also like to point out respect towards wildlife. It is again a natural given; yet again, the lack of respect is visible. Regarding the penguins in the Antarctic, we were told not to approach a penguin ever. If a penguin approached us, we were told to stand still and let the penguin do its ritual of curiosity and exploration. A five-metre rule was established. We were allowed to approach a penguin up to a distance of five metres but then stop. Again, everybody obeyed.

It is, though, logical to learn about wildlife through quiet observations. We don't need to disturb wildlife or plants just for a better look. We can observe wildlife from a distance; we have even got the tools to do so—a binocular or our camera zoom. We do not need to scare them or force them to flee. By the way, quick movements and loud noises are equally as stressful to animals as they are to us human beings. So it is respectful to travel quietly and not pursue, feed, or force animals to flee. There might be one exception to this, and this would be in countries with bears. There, needless to say, it is good to make a little noise so as not to startle the bears. By the way, in hot or cold weather, disturbance can affect an animal's ability to withstand the rigorous environment. Avoid touching, getting close to, feeding, or picking up wild animals as your sign of respect. It is stressful for the animal, and it is possible that the animal may harbour rabies or other diseases.

Allow all animals free access to water sources by giving them the buffer space they need to feel secure. Ideally, you want to put up your camp about two hundred feet away from a water source. Again, in this context, respect goes both ways. Sick or wounded animals can indeed bite, peck, or scratch and hence send you to the hospital. It is also very important for you to let your children specifically know that young animals removed or touched by well-meaning youngsters and adults alike may cause the animals' parents to abandon them. Remember, animals identify by smell. And should you find a sick animal or one in trouble, simply notify a warden or the SPCA.

Yes, all these lessons are learnt—and still, are they put into action? Nature is recently showing us the opposite side of beauty. We heard of bush fires, flooding, tsunamis, and earthquakes with devastating results for the people living in these areas and for their economy. A kind of authority respect emerges. Yes, nature can lead us to think of her as a superior might. In the process of these natural catastrophes, we are starting to *respicere*—to look back at—nature for what it is and from where we all originate in one way or another.

As much as nature can be looked at as a primitive state of existence, untouched and uninfluenced by civilization or artificiality, it can be seen as all natural phenomena, plant, and animal life as distinct from man and his creations. Theology defines nature as humankind's natural state as distinguished from the state of grace. In cell biology, we talk of nature as the processes and functions of the body or any other living creature or plant.

Well, in most cases I witness, we can't really talk of primitive states of existence, as nearly everything on this planet is no longer untouched and has indeed been influenced by civilization and artificiality. And if you look into the function of a single cell, there is certainly no primitivism found in this miracle factory.

A landscape in front of us can seem unspoilt, but if we look a little closer, the human footprint becomes only too visible. All medical and pharmaceutical researches have by now looked into the processes and functions of the cells down to the nucleus, and double standards on how we handle this knowledge are greatly on their way. Standards of basic morality or behaviour are not any longer natural; they are directed, controlled, supervised, and monitored. Instinctual response has lost its appeal.

During my cruise into the Antarctic, I witnessed the make-up of the beauty-and-the-beast aspect of nature close-up. Peril was lurking everywhere in the Antarctic—a continent that is so beautiful, it cannot be described. "Pristine" is the word that comes to my mind—immaculate, nearly unspoiled, nearly untouched, pure, untainted to look at or to *respecere* it. It was serene, tranquil, soothing, marvellous, stunning, spectacular, magnificent, and glorious; at the same time, it was harsh, cruel, malicious, wicked—finding the right word is impossible. It is all of these. It is the beauty and the beast in one package; the beauty cannot exist without the beast, and vice-versa. It is nature as its best. For the first time, I realized fully how judgemental humankind really is. We seem to prefer to only believe in one part of the whole package at a time. In doing so, we destroy the wholeness of the same there and then. We do not give creation the credit or respect it fully deserves, even though as human beings, we are part of the same creation. I was intrigued by this revelation, and it would be with me for some time to come. It also led me to write my book, *Antarctic Revelations and Beyond: The timeless presence of two opposing views*. The two opposing views were the beauty and the beast. I could indeed, for the first time, *respecere*—respect the whole package.

We have to keep an eye on the anonymity and vagueness of our industries offering their packages. Our industries do not respect this very whole package. Our industries are too busy selling to the consumer only one side of their products—the beauty. Rightfully so, I hear them say. After all, we are in for profit.

As much as we teach our children the aforementioned lessons of moral or authority respect, the forces of the anonymity of our industry are unable to make this very desired respect visible to everybody. How then can our children learn?

> Nature is just enough; but men and women must comprehend and accept her suggestions.
>
> **Antoinette Brown Blackwell (1825-1921)**

RESPECT TOWARDS MOTHER NATURE

Mother Nature has shown her self-respect during the last years in manifolds, be it in bushfires, flooding, hurricanes, earthquakes, avalanches, or volcanic eruptions.

In 1999, an earthquake struck in Goluk, Turkey and killed about seventeen thousand people. [*9]

The most famous—and sadly, the most deadly—earthquake hit the US with the San Francisco earthquake in 1906. The estimation was 8.3 on the Richter scale, but worse than the shaking itself, the earthquake caused fires that burned out of control for three days. Two thirds of the city burned down, and the quake totally wiped out the downtown business district. Tens of thousands of people lost their homes and fled the city. About three thousand died. [*10]

During the Depression, the American and Canadian Midwest experienced an eight-year drought. It ruined once-fertile soil and created tremendous dust storms, causing thousands of deaths. The lack of rain left huge areas of farmland without any water. The topsoil was taken up by the wind, creating huge, dark clouds of dust that seemed to turn day into night. People died of starvation and lung diseases caused by breathing in the dust-filled air. Thousands of farmers had to declare bankruptcy. Three hundred fifty thousand people deserted the region. It was the worst drought in North American history. [*11]

China suffered another massive flood from exceptionally heavy rains in 1991. At one point, forty centimetres fell in mere two days. The worst of the flooding was at Tai-Hu, a lake at the mouth of the Yangtze River. The important industrial and agricultural region was devastated. The economic loss and the human toll were costly. Over two thousand people died. In one province, a million homes were simply swept away. Overall, the flood impacted the lives of over two hundred million people. [*11]

The most costly hurricane in American history was Andrew in 1992, which swept through Florida and Louisiana. Fifty-eight people were killed, and so many homes and shops were destroyed, the total cost was at least $27 billion. In terms of dollars, this ranked as the worst natural disaster. [*11]

Because of the media, the worst storm ever to hit the US and Canada in 1993 received its name: "The Storm of the Century." From snow blizzards of arctic air colliding with the warm air from the Gulf of Mexico combined with strong winds and freezing temperatures, it essentially paralyzed the eastern part of the US and Canada. Roofs collapsed, power lines fell, and all major airports closed down. A summary of the damages is 243 deaths and $3 billion. [*11]

The Súðavík Avalanche in Iceland in 1995 killed fourteen people, whereas the Flatyril Avalanche in the same year killed twenty people.

Four years later, in Austria, thirty-one people were killed in the Galtür Avalanche. In 1999, twelve people died with the Montroc Avalanche in France. [12]

Russia made headlines in 2002 when the Kolka-Karmadon rock ice slide caused 125 people to lose their lives to nature. The Flathead Valley avalanches in Canada took eleven lives in 2008. During the year 2009, avalanches happened in Austria, Scotland, Turkey, and Afghanistan and took the lives of thirty-nine people. Pakistan and Afghanistan lost together 274 lives in 2010 in a series of avalanches. [12]

Some of the most significant earthquakes happened in recent times. In 2004, the third largest earthquake in recorded history—the 2004 Indian Ocean earthquake—made headlines by registering a moment magnitude of 9.1-9.3, which triggered huge tsunamis and cost the lives of over 230,000 people. [13] The July 2006 Java earthquake with a magnitude of 7.7 also triggered tsunamis. Five hundred forty-seven people lost their lives to this earthquake, five hundred ninety five people were recorded injured, two hundred seventy five went missing, and 54,256 people were displaced. [14] The 2005 earthquake in Kashmir was a major one centred in Pakistan measuring 7.6, similar in size to the 1906 San Francisco earthquake. The official death toll counted 75,000. [15] In May 2008, the Sichuan earthquake followed in the Chinese province of Sichuan with a registered magnitude of 7.9. The death toll stood at 69,197. The earthquake also affected countries in the surrounding regions. Tremors were felt in Tajikistan, western China, while officials said nearly 1,400 also died in India/Kashmir and four people in Afghanistan. The severity of the damage caused by nature this way was attributed to severe up thrust coupled with poor construction. [16] The 2010 Chile earthquake with a magnitude of 8.8 triggered another tsunami and cost 525 lives not counting those who lost their lives in the aftershocks and widespread tsunamis. [17]

2011 topped the most recent earthquakes with a magnitude of 9.0 in Tohoku, Japan. This was an undersea mega thrust quake off the coast of Japan with its epicentre about seventy kilometres east of the Oshika Peninsula of Tohoku and the hypocentre at an underwater depth of only around thirty-two kilometres. It remains the most powerful known earthquake to have hit Japan so far and one of the five most powerful earthquakes in the world overall since modern record-keeping began early in 1900. The Island of Honshu was moved eight feet eastward. The earthquake triggered extremely destructive tsunami waves of up to 40.5 metres in Miyako, Iwate, and Tohoku. In some cases, the waves travelled up to ten kilometres inland. In addition to loss of life and destruction of infrastructure, the tsunami caused a number of nuclear accidents, primarily the ongoing level seven meltdowns at three reactors in Fukushima I Nuclear Power Plant complex and the associated evacuation zones, affecting hundreds of thousands of residents.

The Japanese Prime Minister, Naoto Kan, said, "In the sixty-five years after the end of World War II, this is the toughest and the most difficult crisis for Japan." [18] The Japanese National Police Agency confirmed 15,844 deaths, 5,890 injuries, and 3,451 people missing across eighteen prefectures as well as over 125,000 buildings damaged or destroyed. [19] The quake along with the tsunami caused extensive and severe structural damages for the country, including heavy damages to roads and railways as well as fires in many areas, and a dam collapsed on top of all that. Around 4.4 million households in northeaster Japan were left without electricity, and 1.5 million were without water. Many electrical generators had to be taken down, and at least three nuclear reactors suffered explosions due to the hydrogen gas that had built up with their out containment buildings after cooling system failure. Residents within a twenty-metre radius of the Fukushima I Nuclear Power Plant and a ten-kilometre radius of the Fukushima II Nuclear Power Plant were evacuated. In addition, the US recommended that its citizens evacuate up to eighty kilometres outside the plant. Early estimates placed insured losses from the earthquake alone at $14.5 to $34.6 billion (USD). The Bank of Japan offered ¥15 trillion (an equivalent to $183 billion USD) to the banking system on 14 March in an effort to normalize conditions. The overall cost could exceed the $300 billion (USD) mark, making it the most expensive natural disaster on record. On top of all of this, the earthquake in Japan moved Honshu 2.4 metres east and shifted the earth on its axis by estimates of between ten and twenty-five centimetres. Twelve thousand people are still missing. [19]

The Japanese earthquake makes all facets of a pluralistic socioeconomic society transparent once hit by a natural disaster of such magnitude. Mother Nature is exercising her rights for equilibrium, and societies lay helpless at her feet. Equilibrium is the condition of any system in biology, physics, chemistry or other sciences in which competing influences of all interdependent parts are thriving for balance.

It was no surprise to me when I heard end of August, 2011, that the Japanese Prime Minister, Naoto Kan, announced his resignation and Yoshihiko Noda from the Democratic Party of Japan was formally appointed as Prime Minister by the Emperor of Japan beginning September of 2011. He is known to be a hard worker for his people and is determined to move politics forward.

Floods have also made a lot of headlines this year and are always a disastrous reminder of Mother Nature's power. The Great Flood of 1993 was one of the most costly floods in United States history. It occurred in the American Midwest along the mighty Mississippi and Missouri rivers and their tributaries from April to October 1993. It was considered to be the most costly and devastating flood to ever have occurred in the US, causing $15 billion in damages. The hydro-graphic basin affected covered a total of about 320,000 square kilometres. Within this zone, the flooded area totalled around 38,000 square kilometres and became known as the worst US disaster since the Great Mississippi Flood of 1927, as measured by duration, square miles inundated, persons displaced, crop and property damage, and number of record river levels.

In some categories, the 1993 flood even surpassed the 1927 flood, which at the time was the largest flood ever recorded on the Mississippi.

Some locations on the Mississippi River flooded for almost two hundred days, while various locations on the Missouri experienced 100 days of flooding. Residents of Grafton in Illinois were flooded for 195 days; Clarksville, Missouri for 187 days; Winfield, Missouri for 183 days; Hannibal, Missouri for 174 days; and in Quincy, Illinois for 152 days. The Missouri River was above flood stage for sixty-two days in Jefferson City, seventy-seven days in Hermann, and ninety-four days in St. Charles in the St. Louis metropolitan area. Finally, on 7 October 7, 103 days after the flooding began, the Mississippi River at St. Louis finally dropped below flood stage. About 100,000 homes were destroyed and fifteen million acres of farmland inundated. The whole towns of Valmeyer, Illinois and Rhineland, Missouri had to be relocated to higher grounds. The floods cost thirty-two lives officially, but a more likely target is suspected to be around fifty people as well as an estimated $15-20 billion in damages. Even after the water was gone, billions of pounds of sand covered homes and farms. [*20]

In 1998, the Yangtze River floods in China left fifteen million people homeless. The flood lasted from middle of June to the beginning of September. This was considered the worst Northern flood in forty years. Three thousand seventy-four people were counted dead, and the economic loss was estimated at $26 billion. Other sources reported a total loss of 4,150 people, with 180 million people being otherwise affected in one or another way. One hundred thousand square kilometres had to be evacuated, and 13.3 million houses were damaged or destroyed. [*21]

In 2000, the Limpopo River in South Mozambique flooded much of the country for weeks, resulting in thousands of deaths and leaving the country devastated for years to come. It was a truly natural disaster that occurred in February and March of 2000, with heavy rainfall lasting for five weeks and making many homeless. Around eight hundred people died. One thousand four hundred square kilometres of arable land was affected, and 20,000 head of cattle were lost. It was considered to be the worst flood in the Mozambique in fifty years. Over 45,000 people were rescued from rooftops, trees, and other isolated areas. The first rescue efforts were carried out by only a few Mozambique naval vessels. The governments of South Africa, Malawi, and Mozambique provided only a few helicopters to the rescue team. A woman with the name of Sofia Pedro will not forget this day; she gave birth in a tree while surrounded by flood waters. She was then rescued by the South African Air Force, which flew both her and the newborn daughter, Rositha, to Chibuto. This brief snippet of just one person's experience may seem out of place among all the statistics. But I would like to remind the reader that every statistic in this chapter relates in one way or another to the fate of one single person.

Mozambique is not the US, and infrastructure as well as given logistics resulted in only slow rescue actions, including those offered by international aid organizations. Only three weeks after the onset of the flood, significant rescue equipment arrived from Europe and North America. After being isolated with families on islands, some of the children died from starvation. Ninety percent of the country's functioning irrigation infrastructure was damaged, causing the worst of agriculture losses suffered. Six hundred thirty schools were closed, leaving 2,124,000 students and teachers without classrooms. Forty-two health units were destroyed, including the Beira Central Hospital, the second largest in the country. The Mozambique government requested $450 million in international aid at a donor conference held in Rome in early May 2000. [22]

In 2005, the Mumbai floods followed. This event became more known as the 2005 Maharashtra floods, when many parts of the Indian state of Maharashtra—including large parts of the metropolis of Mumbai—were flooded. Mumbai is a city on the coast of the Arabian Sea on the western coast of India in which at least five thousand people died. The flooding happened just one month after the June 2005 Gujarat floods. July 26 is now understood in the context for the day when Mumbai came to a standstill. Large numbers of people were stranded on the road. Several lost their homes, and many walked for long distances back home from work that evening. The floods were caused by the eighth heaviest ever recorded twenty-four-hour rainfall figure of 994 millimetres, which lashed the metropolis on 26 July, 2005. Intermittently, the rainfall continued the next day, and 644 millimetres were received within the twelve-hour period between 8:00 a.m. and 8:00 p.m. that day.

Torrential rainfall continued for the next week. The highest rainfall in a twenty-four-hour period in India was 1.168 millimetres in Aminidivi in the Union Territory of Lakshadweep in May 2004, although some reports suggested that it was a new Indian record. A previous record high rainfall in the same period for Mumbai was 575 millimetres in 1974. Raigad, Chiplun, Khed, Ratnagiri and Kalvan in Maharashtra and the southern state of Goa were severely affected by the 2005 floods. The rains lessened between 28 July and 30 July but picked up in intensity again on 31 July. The Maharashtra State government declared 27 July and 28 July as a state holiday for all affected areas and also ordered all schools in those regions to close on 1-2 August. The Mumbai police commissioner requested all residents to stay indoors as far as possible on 31 July after heavy rains disrupted the city once again. The commissioner grounded all flights for the day as well.

The detailed reporting of the 2005 Mumbai floods makes the scale of the overall devastation and disruption to people living in such environment when Mother Nature shows her ugly face only too transparent. Thousands of school children were stranded and could not reach home for up to twenty-four hours. It was mere a measure of respect for children and parents alike to have the following two days declared as school and college holidays by the state government.

But the rains also impacted the State of Goa and some parts of western Maharashtra on 25 July. Adding to the chaos was the lack of public information. Radio stations and many television stations did not receive any weather warnings or alerts by the civic agencies. In hindsight, the Met Department blamed it on the lack of sophisticated weather radars, which would have given at least a three-hour prior warning due to high tides.

In floods of this scale, the threat to public health is imminent. The rain water caused sewage systems to overflow, and all water lines became contaminated. The government ordered all housing societies to add chlorine to their water tanks. Thousands of animal carcasses started to float in the flood waters, raising concerns about the possibility of disease. Reports in the media warned of possible waterborne diseases, and hospitals and health centres alike geared up to distribute free medicine to manage any outbreak.

India, though considered poor in many areas, has sufficient commercial, trading, and industrial activities around the country, mostly in the higher-populated areas. The financial cost of these floods was unprecedented. The floods caused a stoppage of all commercial and industrial activities for days. Preliminary indications indicated that the floods caused a direct loss of about RS 450 crores, which equal around €80 million or $100 million (USD). For a country like India, this is a lot, and the financial impact was manifested in a variety of ways. The banking transactions across the counters were adversely affected, and many branches and commercial establishments were unable to function from late evening of 26 July. Again, as a sign of respect, the state government declared 27 and 28 July as public holidays.

ATM networks of several banks—including the State Bank of India, the nation's biggest national bank; ICICI Bank; the HDFC Bank; and several foreign banks like Citibank and HSBC—stopped functioning from the afternoon of 26 July. ATM transactions could not be carried out in several parts of India for two days due to failure of connectivity with their central systems located in Mumbai. The Bombay Stock Exchange and the National Stock Exchange of India, the premier stock exchanges of India, could only partially function. As most of the trading is so-called e-trading, trading terminals of the brokerage houses across the country remained largely inoperative. Whilst the exchanges remained closed for 29 July, ironically, in partial trading, the SENSEX—India's most-tracked equity index—closed at an all-time high of 7605.03 on 27 July.

Needless to say, the 2005 Mumbai floods had wide-ranging effects on the rest of the world. For the first time ever, Mumbai's domestic and international airports—Chatrapati Shivaji International, Sahar, and Juhu Aerodrome—were shut for more than thirty hours due to heavy flooding of the runways alongside extremely poor visibility. Over seven hundred flights were cancelled or delayed. The airports reopened on the morning of 28 July. Within twenty-four hours of airports becoming operational again, there were 185 departures registered and 184 arrivals, including international flights. Again from the early morning of 31 July, with an increase in water logging of the runways and different parts of Mumbai, most of the flights were indefinitely cancelled.

Rail links also became disrupted. On the late evening of 30 July reports talked of the cancellation of several long-distance trains up to 6 August, 2005. In all, fifty-two local trains were damaged. The Mumbai Pune Expressway—or officially, the Yashwantrao Chavan Expressway—had several landslides and had to be closed the first time ever in its history for twenty-four hours. Thirty-seven thousand Indian typical auto-rickshaws were spoilt, four thousand taxis, and nine hundred of the BEST buses were damaged. Ten thousand trucks, including tempos, had to be grounded.

According to the *Hindustan Times,* an unprecedented five million mobile line and 2.3 million MTNL landline users were been hit for over four hours. And according to the personal communication registrar, the DNS servers in Mumbai had to be reconfigured because the servers were not operational.

Which factors in Mumbai aggravated the disaster caused by Mother Nature's moods? Did her human species fail to see what power she really is able to show? In hindsight, India's storm water drainage specialists now know more. The then-present storm water drainage system in Mumbai was put in place in the early twentieth century and was capable of carrying only twenty-five millimetres of water per hour. This, of course, was extremely inadequate on a day when 993 millimetres fell from the heavens. The drainage system was also clogged at several places; this was found out when it was too late. Only three so-called outfalls (ways out to the sea) were equipped with floodgates, whereas a remaining 102 opened directly into the sea. As a result, there was no way to stop seawater from rushing into the drainage system during high tide.

A very ambitious plan was drawn early in 1990 to overhaul the city's storm water drainage system. It had not been reviewed in over fifty years. The Brihanmumbai Municipal Corporation had hired UK-based consultants to study the matter and a project costing around 600 crore rupees was proposed. Implementation of the project could have ensured that rainwater did not flood the streets of Mumbai. The project was planned for completion by 2002 and had also aimed to enhance the drainage system through larger-diameter storm water drains and pipes using pumps wherever necessary and removing encroachments. This project could have doubled the storm water carrying capacity to fifty millimetres per hour. But (when it comes to money, there's always a "but") the BMC committee rejected the proposed projects on the grounds that it was too costly. The city of Mumbai suffered gravely with the 2005 Mumbai floods—again due to the playgrounds of a pluralistic socioeconomic society. [*23]

Money does not have eyes; money cannot look at *(respecere)* anything. It remains largely blind towards matters of respect. I think this example shows that Mother Nature does not have to earn respect; she simply deserves respect. And it is a society with all its individuals that has to earn her respect.

There is more to blame for the Mumbai disaster. Unlike South Mumbai, developments in the northern suburbs of Mumbai are completed. In hindsight, they were known to have been constructed without proper planning. The Environment Ministry of the Government in India, so it is said, had been informed in the early 1990s that sanctioning the Bandra Kurla complex, a commercial complex in northern Mumbai, could well lead to disaster. But no environmental clearance was mandatory for large urban construction projects in northern Mumbai. Officials in the environment Ministry claimed that it was not practical to impose new guidelines with retrospective effect, as there are millions of buildings. Well, the question again is this: who deserves respect, and who has to earn it?

In 2010, the media reported on the Pakistan floods damaging crops and infrastructure and claiming many lives. These floods began in late July 2010 and were caused by heavy monsoon rains in the Khyber Pakhtunkhwa, Sindh, Punjab and Balochistan regions of Pakistan. They affected the Indus River basin. Near to one fifth of Pakistan's total land area was underwater—796,095 square kilometres. According to the Pakistani government data, the floods directly impacted about twenty million people—mostly by destruction of property, livelihood, and infrastructure—with a death toll of close to two thousand. [*24]

Floods certainly do show their perils to humankind—and all living creatures, for that matter—in a wide range of destruction and damage. They are not always just caused by rainfalls or monsoon seasons. Tropical cyclones can result in extensive flooding and storm surges, as happened with Hurricane Katrina, which devastated the Gulf Coast of the US around New Orleans in Louisiana in 2005, Cyclone Yasi in 2011 in Australia, and just recently, Hurricane Irene in August 2011. All had a catastrophic impact on humans, animals, infrastructure, logistics, commerce, trade, and other exchange activities. Though the loss of people seems to diminish compared to flooding disasters of more than twenty years ago, the loss of lifestyle and comfort seems comparatively harder to cope with than ever before.

Other huge flooding disasters yet again are caused by tsunamis triggered by earthquakes. In 2010, two major earthquakes triggering tsunamis happened in Chile and Indonesia. The Chile earthquake triggered a tsunami, which devastated several coastal towns in south central Chile and damaged the port at Talcahuano. But tsunami warnings were issued in fifty-three countries. The tsunami's waves caused minor damage in the San

Diego area of California and the Tohoku region of Japan, where damage to the fishery business was estimated at ¥ 6.26 billion (the equivalent of $66.7 million USD). The Chile earthquake also generated a blackout that affected 93 percent of the country's population, continuing for several days in some locations. The death toll was calculated at 562, compared with earlier estimates of 802. [25]

The October 2010 Sumatra earthquake was of magnitude 7.7 and happened on the same fault line that produced the 2004 Indian Ocean earthquake. It resulted in a substantial localized tsunami in the Mentawai Islands. Many villages were affected by the tsunami, which reached a height of three metres and swept as far as six hundred metres inland. The tsunami caused widespread destruction, displacing more than twenty thousand people on its way and affecting about four thousand households. Reportedly, 435 people were killed, but over 100 remained missing. [26]

Mother Nature's seasonal moods also bring blizzards. They are severe winter storms with low temperature, strong winds, and heavy snow. The difference between a blizzard and a snow storm is the strength of the wind. To become a typical blizzard, a storm must show winds in excess of thirty-five miles per hour, reduce visibility to 0.25 miles, and last for a prolonged period of three hours or more. Ground blizzards require high winds to stir up snow that has already fallen rather than fresh snowfall.

Blizzards always have a negative impact on local economics and can completely terminate visibility in regions where snowfall is rare. A significant blizzard occurred in Afghanistan in 2008.

It was fierce and record-breaking. Temperatures fell to a low of 30⁰ C, with up to 180 centimetres of snow in the more mountainous regions. Nine hundred twenty-six people were reported dead. Hospitals performed frostbite amputations on at least 100 people across the country, as many had walked barefoot in freezing cold mud and snow. The severe weather conditions also claimed the lives of more than one hundred thousand sheep and goats and nearly 315,000 cattle. [27]

In Mother Nature's treasure chest are also droughts and heat waves. As of 2006, states of Australia—including South Australia, Western Australia, New South Wales, Northern Territory and Queensland—were under severe drought conditions for five to ten years in a row. The drought is now beginning to affect urban area populations for the first time. The majority of the country is under strict water restrictions.

To define drought in Australia for the purpose of political and socioeconomic measures to come into force, we have to think of a rainfall over a three-month period being in the lowest decile of what has been recorded for that specific region in the past. This definition takes into account that drought is a relative term, and rainfall deficiencies need to be compared to typical rainfall patterns, including those of seasonal variations. Other factors than rainfall can also be taken into consideration depending on a state's government view.

The 2000s drought in Australia has been declared the worst since settlement. This drought began in 1995 and continued until late 2009. Needless to say, drought has changed the way Australians treat their water resources. Long-term effects of the drought showed between 2006 and 2007, and many state governments have attempted to drought-proof their states with more permanent solutions. In the past hundred years, Australia as a country had solely relied on water from dams for agriculture and consumption. But now, new measures have come into effect, such as grey water recycling, government rebates for home owners who install water tanks, and tougher restrictions on industries.

People in Australia eventually awakened to Mother Nature's talents and have begun to respect these in response. For example, the residents of Toowoomba initially voted on (and rejected) a referendum on using recycled sewerage water. However, soon after the referendum, Toowoomba had to begin using recycled sewerage water, as no other feasible alternative was available. Brisbane has been set to be supplied via larger dams, a pipeline, and possibly also recycling. On the Gold Coast in Queensland, a desalination project could be initiated, whereas plans for a similar project in Sydney were halted with great public opposition and with a discovery of underground aquifers. Yes, Australia now is learning and is in the process of starting to respect Mother Nature.

An aquifer is an underground layer of water bearing permeable rock or unconsolidated materials—such as gravel, sand, or silt—from which groundwater can be usefully extracted using water wells. Sydney's science specialists now are learning hydrogeology—the study of water flow in and the characterization of aquifers. In November 2006, Perth completed a seawater desalination plant to supply the city with 17 percent of its needs. Likewise, the Victorian government in the South of Australia has started building one of the world's largest desalination plants. Upon completion, it should have the capability to produce up to a third of Melbourne's water needs.

Australian dairy producers have been hit particularly hard by the drought. The year 2004 stood out as a very bleak year for them, as the drought conditions caused production to be down by 4.5 percent. The agriculture production had been affected largely. Australia's cotton industry alone showed a drop, with the smallest areas planted in twenty years and a 66 percent reduction compared to five years prior. The crop was half its usual size for three of the past five years. Water use by the industry fell by 3.7 percent between 2000 and 2005, mainly due to drought. Twenty cotton communities—mainly in New South Wales, where ten thousand people were directly employed in this industry—were severely impacted. Stock feed, of course, was getting scarce, and farmers who were equally affected found it hard to feed their cattle and sheep.

Most Australian mainland capital cities have been facing a major water crisis for quite some time, with less than 50 percent of water storages remaining. Melbourne, for instance, had rain up to 90 percent below the average for September and October 2006, compounding the problem of extremely low rainfall from the preceding winter months. Melbourne experienced high temperatures throughout October 2006, which has caused evaporation of water in dams and reservoirs. As a result, water levels fell by around 0.1 percent per day. As a result, Melbourne has been put on even tighter water restrictions. As of July 2009, water levels in dams were at a mere 27 percent of capacity.

Back in early 2007, weather forecasters predicted that the drought would ease along the east coast with a return to average rainfall from late February 2007. They believed that the El Niño effect that had been rampant during 2006 and 2007 had ended. A heavy rainfall during June and July in the coastal areas of New South Wales and in Victoria's Gippsland region, together with tentative forecasts of La Niña, brought a lot of hope that the draught might end. John Howard, the Prime Minister at the time, announced in mid-April 2007 that unless there was substantial rain in the next six weeks, no water could be allocated to irrigators in the Murray-Darling basin for the next coming year. The result could have directly affected fifty thousand farmers and the economy. And if the Snowy Mountain Scheme would have been forced to shut down its hydroelectric generators, an electricity shortage may have been another problem.

The Darling River flowed again, however, after nearly a year of no flows. Inflows into the Murray Darling Basin in the winter of 2007 were reported amongst the lowest on record, although marginally better than those of the previous winter during 2006.The drought in Sydney eased around April 2008 when the city's main water catchments reached 65 percent (25 percent fuller than it had been at the same time during the previous year). Victoria, however, remained drought-affected. Melbourne's water supplies dipped to around 30 percent by July 2008. Drought conditions in Tasmania worsened in 2008, with many regions reporting no significant rainfall for three years.

In 2009, the severe drought conditions in South East Australia continued after one of the driest summers for the region. Melbourne had had Stage 3a water restrictions form April 2007 and narrowly avoided Stage 4 restrictions, with the minimum storage level of around 25.8 percent remaining above the threshold of 25 percent for enacting Stage 4. Many towns in Victoria were close to running out of water, with some of the few Victorian townships without water restrictions being in the East Gippsland water area, where reservoir levels were above 80 percent. The 2010 Victorian storms did very little to help Melbourne's storage levels. Luckily, steady rain and the Victorian floods of the same year in September caused the storage levels to remain above about 32.7 percent, rising to over 46 percent in September and 51 percent by late November.

2010 was Australia's wettest spring on record due to a moderate to strong La Nina event developing over the region. Water restrictions could be reduced to stage 3 on 2 April and stage 2 on 1 September. 2010 was also Melbourne's wettest spring since 1993, with Melbourne reaching an average annual rainfall in 2010.

The drought in Queensland had mostly eased with Brisbane's very heavy rain in May 2009, and Premier Anna Bligh announced that South East Queensland was no longer experiencing drought. Brisbane's dams are now at full capacity, with the state in general experiencing its wettest spring on record. Luckily, the drought in New South Wales has also eased. In the beginning of 2010, the percentage of the state in drought was pushing 70 percent. As of the end of the year, the entire state was officially out of drought and experienced its wettest spring on record. Several rivers—even those in the outback—had flooded several times, and many dams were overflowing, including the Burrendong, Burrinjuck, and Pindari Dams. Canberra's dams reached a level above 90 percent. But despite Western Australia having to endure its fifth wettest spring on record, in the South West, Gascoyne, and Pilbara regions of Western Australia, the drought had, in fact, intensified. This area recorded its driest year on record. The dam of Perth registered its lowest inflows on record, with Perth itself registering its third driest year on record along with the hottest spring ever recorded.

The Australian environmental movement organization, Sustainable Population Australia, contended that as the driest inhabited continent, Australia could not continue to sustain its current rate of population growth without becoming overpopulated. The SPA also argued that climate change could lead to deterioration of natural ecosystems through increased temperatures, extreme weather events, and less rainfall in the southern parts of the continent, thus reducing its capacity to sustain a large population even further. In response to this, Australia witnessed several movements and campaigns around the country advocating for a responsible environmental action. Despite the fact that Australia looks like a vast and nearly empty continent on the surface, a UK-based Optimum Population Trust supported the view that Australia was overpopulated and believed that the optimum population should be ten million rather than the present of about twenty-one million, with a fairly reduced standard of living. [*28]

Where there's a drought, there's fire. Wildfires are much-uncontrolled fires burning in wild land areas, with common causes being lightning and drought. Unfortunately, Mother Nature is not always to blame. Wildfires could also be started by simple human negligence or by arson. Of course, if we would include the human species into the category of Mother Nature, then we still could blame her, as well. I argue that the human species is as much part of Mother Nature as the animal and plant species on our planet, including all living organisms. Science more and more has reached the conclusion that, indeed, everything comes down to a molecular source of existence, no matter if human, animal, plant, or organism.

Let's talk about the 2009 Victorian bushfire in Australia, which also became known as the Black Saturday bushfire. It was, in fact, a series of bushfires which ignited or were burning across the state of Victoria on and around 7 February, 2009. The fire occurred during extreme bushfire weather conditions and resulted in Australia's highest ever loss of life from a bushfire, with 173 people dead and 414 injured as a result of these fires. As many as four hundred individual fires were recorded on this Black Saturday. The majority of these fires ignited and spread on a day that was 40° C and had wind speeds in excess of 100 kilometres per hour. Taking into consideration that there had been no rain for almost two months, the fires could easily fan over large distances.

Around Melbourne, the firestorms accounted for 120 of the 173 deaths in total. Then a cool change hit the state in the early evening hours, bringing with it gale force south-westerly winds of more than 120 kilometres per hour. And it was this change in wind direction that had caused the long eastern flanks of the fires to become massive fire fronts that burnt with incredible speed and ferocity towards towns that had earlier escaped the fires. Two thousand thirty homes were destroyed as well as 3,500 structures in total, with thousands of buildings suffering severe damages. The fires affected seventy-eight individual townships in total and displaced an estimated 7,562 people. Many displaced people had to seek temporary accommodation, and much of these had been donated in the form of spare rooms, caravans, tents, and beds in community relief centres. [29]

The majority of the fires were, in fact, caused by fallen or clashing power lines or were deliberately lit. Other suspected the ignition source to be lightening, cigarette butts, or sparks from power tools. Only by early to mid-March did favourable conditions finally aid containment efforts and help extinguish the fires.

In the context of Mother Nature's might, I also like to mention the worst drought recorded in modern times. Nearly eight million people and over seven million cattle had to face water shortages in the Sichuan Province of China in 2006. Reportedly, more than seventeen million people in Southwest China's Chongqing Municipality and the neighbouring Sichuan Province were tortured by a serious lack of adequate drinking water due to ongoing droughts and searing heat. The month-long droughts affected fourteen million people in forty countries in Chongqing, and 6.1 million ran out of drinking water. Temperatures in Sichuan stayed above 38⁰ C, with climbs up to 42.8 degrees. Crops on large tracts of farmland withered up, and many regions had no harvests at all. The droughts caused an estimated economic loss of 9.23 billion Yuan, which equals about $1.15 billion (USD) in only two regions of the affected areas. [*30]

Heat has become a matter of headlines more than ever before. In 2003, the European Heat Wave was recorded as the hottest summer on record in Europe since at least 1540. France was hit especially hard. The heat wave led to a health crisis in several countries and combined with drought to create a crop shortfall in southern Europe. More than forty thousand Europeans died as a result of this heat wave. Portugal experienced extensive forest fires. Five percent of the countryside and 10 percent of the forests were destroyed—a total of 215,000 hectares or four thousand square kilometres. Eighteen people died in the fires, but there were an estimated 1,866-2,039 heat-related deaths overall. Temperatures reached as high as 48⁰ C.

The Netherlands reported 1,500 heat-related deaths, largely within the population of the elderly. The highest temperature recorded this heat wave was on 7 August. In Limburg, a temperature of 37.8°C was reached—0.8⁰ C below the national record since 1704. It happened only twice that a higher temperature was recorded. On 8 August, a temperature of 37.7⁰ C was recorded, and 12 August saw a temperature of 37.2°C.

Spain recorded 141 deaths, and temperature records were broken in various cities, including 45.1⁰ C in Jerez. Record temperatures were reached in most cities between 36⁰ C and 45.2⁰ C.

The summer of 2003 in Italy was the warmest in the last three centuries, and the maximum temperatures of July and August remained above 30⁰ C, whereas Sicily reached an absolute maximum of 46⁰ Celsius.

In Germany, a record temperature of 40.4⁰ C was recorded in Bavaria, but some experts argue that the upper Rhine plain would have received the highest temperatures—over 41⁰ C. With only half the normal rainfall, rivers were at their lowest this century, and shipping could not navigate the rivers Elbe or Danube. Around three hundred people, mostly the elderly, died during the 2003 heat wave in Germany alone. In the neighbouring Switzerland, a new nationwide temperature of 41.5⁰ C was recorded, and melting glaciers in the Alps caused avalanches and flash floods.

As well, the United Kingdom was in general suffering from a warm summer, with temperatures well above average. However, the Atlantic cyclones brought cool and wet weather for a short while at the end of July and beginning of August to give the population a break. But then temperatures started to increase substantially once more, and several weather records were broken. The highest temperature was recorded at Brogdale orchards in Kent with 38.5⁰ C, in London with 38⁰ C, and in Greycrook near the Scottish borders with 32.9⁰ C. The BBC reported around two thousand deaths during the 2003 heat wave, most people of these being over eighty years of age.

But the heat not only showed its peril towards people, but also towards crops all over Europe—mostly in southern Europe. France suffered 20 percent shortfalls in wheat harvests as a result of the long drought, Italy 13 percent, the United Kingdom 12 percent, the Ukraine 75 percent, and Moldova 80 percent. Many other countries had shortfalls of between 5 and 10 percent in wheat harvest, and the EU total production was down by ten million tonnes, or 10 percent. The heat wave also greatly accelerated the ripening of grapes. Heat dehydrates grapes and makes for more concentrated juice. By mid-August, the grapes in certain vineyards had already reached their normal sugar content, possibly resulting in 12⁰ and 12.5⁰ alcoholic wines. Because of that (and also the impending change to rainy weather), the grape harvest had to start much earlier than usual. The normal harvesting time would have been September compared with early harvesting in mid-August. One sunny side for wine makers became transparent. It was predicted that the wines from 2003 would have exceptional quality, especially in France, even if we only can talk in scarce quantity. Hungary was lucky, though. The heat wave made very well for them in the Vinalies 2003 International wine contest. A total of nine gold and nine silver medals were awarded to Hungarian winemakers.

The anomalous overheating during the European summer of 2003 also affected the atmosphere and created anomalies on sea surface stratification in the Mediterranean Sea as well as on the surface currents. The Atlantic Ionia Stream, a seasonal current of the Central Mediterranean Sea, was affected by the warm temperatures and modified its path and intensity. Specialists have suggested that the heat waves may have influenced the stock of important pelagic commercial fish species in their biological reproduction. Further studies are on their way. [*31]

Again in 2010, the Northern Hemisphere summer resulted in severe heat waves, which killed over two thousand people. It not only resulted in hundreds of wildfires, causing widespread air pollution, but also burned thousands of square miles of forest. Impacted were most of the United States, Kazakhstan, Mongolia, China, Hong Kong, North Africa, and the European continent as a whole along with parts of Canada, Russia, Indochina, South Korea, and Japan during the months of May through August of 2010. Its worst was felt in June over the eastern United States, Middle East, eastern Europe, European Russia, northeastern China, and southeastern Russia.

Incidentally, June 2010 marked the fourth consecutive warmest month on record globally at 0.66^0 C above average, while the period of April through June was the warmest ever recorded for land areas in the Northern Hemisphere at 1.25^0 C above average. The previous record for the global average temperature for the month of June was set in 2005 at 0.66^0 C, with the previous warm record for April through June over Northern Hemisphere land areas had been 1.16^0 C above average in 2007. The weather caused forest fires in China, where three in a team of three hundred died fighting a fire in the Binchuan county of Dali. Yunnan suffered the worst drought in sixty years by 17 February. A major drought was reported as early as January across the Sahel. In August, a section of the Petermann Glacier tongue connecting northern Greenland, the Nares Strait, and the Arctic Ocean broke off; this was the biggest ice shelf in the Arctic to detach in forty-eight years.[32]

Let this all be Mother Nature's might. It might even be human involvement that caused heat waves, droughts, or flooding. The World Meteorological Organization argued that all of these events did fit with predictions based on global warning for the twenty-first century. However, they also said that no specific weather events could be linked directly to climate change. Some climatologists still insist that these weather events almost definitely would not have happened if the atmospheric carbon dioxide was at pre-industrial levels.

Are we not respecting Mother Nature's might? Has industrialization along with corporate greed made human beings so ignorant that they themselves have lost respect for themselves, not seeing that at the molecular foundation of existence, we are indeed a part of Mother Nature? I wonder.

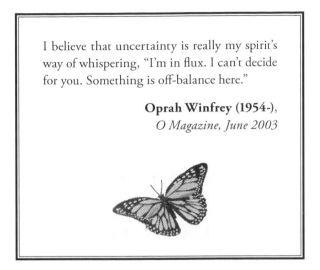

I believe that uncertainty is really my spirit's way of whispering, "I'm in flux. I can't decide for you. Something is off-balance here."

Oprah Winfrey (1954-),
O Magazine, June 2003

RESPECT TOWARDS THE UNIVERSE

As we are talking Mother Nature, we also have to mention tornadoes, or twisters—violent, dangerous, rotating columns of air that are in contact with both the surface of the earth and a cumulonimbus cloud or, in some cases, the base of a cumulus cloud. While I was living in Texas, I learnt that tornadoes came in many shapes and sizes but were typically in the form of a visible condensation funnel whose narrow end touched the earth and was often encircled by a cloud of debris and dust—a rather amazing picture to witness despite a very looming danger.

Most tornadoes can have wind speeds less than 117 kilometres per hour, can be around eighty metres across, and can travel a few kilometres before dissipating. The most extreme can attain wind speeds of more than 480 kilometres per hour, stretch more than 3 kilometres, across and can stay on the ground for more than 100 kilometres. I would like to only mention those that occurred during 2011.

As of 24 August 2011, there have been 1,718 tornadoes reported in the US alone, of which at least 1,239 were confirmed [33] 2011 so far has been an exceptionally destructive and deadly year for tornadoes worldwide with at least 566 people perishing due to their appearance: twelve in Bangladesh, one in New Zealand, one in the Philippines, one in Russia, one in Canada, and an estimate of 550 in the United States, compared to 564 US deaths in the ten years prior combined.

Due in large part to several extremely large tornado outbreaks in the middle and end of April and in late May, 2011 is currently on near record pace, with six EF5 tornadoes as of 6 July. It also has been the deadliest year for tornadoes in the US since 1936, mostly due to the 324 tornadic deaths that occurred during the 27 April outbreak across the southeastern United States and the 150 tornadic deaths that resulted from the 2011 Joplin Tornado.

At late season, deadly tornado outbreaks continued through the early hours of 1 January, 2011, with seven tornadoes touching down in Mississippi over three hours. The strongest of these, rated EF3 with winds of 233 kilometres per hour, reached 1.21 kilometres in width along its 37.74 kilometre track and caused significant damage all along the Mississippi Highway 19. Structures were damaged and destroyed, and two people were injured. Near Mississippi Highway 35, thousands of trees were uprooted. Another EF3 touched down near Macon, damaging and destroying more structures and injuring one person. The overall damage in the state from tornadoes amounted to $10.4 million.

Then, in late January, three more tornadoes touched down in Eastern Europe—two in Turkey and one in Greece. The F1 tornado in Turkey caused the wall of an industrial building to collapse, and other structures sustained roof damage. The strongest, an F2 tornado, touched down in the north of Rhodes and destroyed small structures in its path, killing several heads of cattle. In some places, hail fell up to five centimetres in diameter, damaging farmland and greenhouses. Accumulations of hail had also reached fifteen centimetres in the Mersin Province of Turkey. Several tornadoes followed down across parts of the US in February of 2011. The most significant was in the south eastern part of Nashville in Tennessee. Significant damage could be reported near the Hickory Hollow Mall as well as near Percy Priest Lake during the evening hours, with widespread wind damage all across Middle Tennessee. A tornado emergency was declared shortly thereafter for regions to the north east in Wilson Country, where another tornado raged, causing further injuries. Both tornadoes were rated EF2.

More tornadoes touched down with varying degrees of damage in the Missouri Bootheel, west Tennessee, Mississippi, southwestern Kentucky, and parts of Arkansas, including three more reported of rating EF2. Another severe weather event developed on 27 February and continued into 28 February across the Midwest and South. At least thirty-five tornadoes were reported across several states, but a large portion of the damages occurred due to damaging straight line winds. The most destructive EF2 tornado was in Franklin County of Tennessee, being the first killer tornado of 2011 on the afternoon of 28 February in which one person was killed. Another EF3-rated tornado destroyed houses near Eminence in Kentucky, and further concentrated tornado activity by late February occurred in parts of Missouri and Illinois with altogether twenty-two tornadoes in the region. Some were as strong as EF2 with a series of squall lines in which further tornadoes were embedded. (A squall line is a line of severe thunderstorms which can form along and ahead of a cold front.) But none of those resulted in any fatalities.

During the first week of March, one confirmed EF0 tornado hit Crowley in Louisiana, whereas another hit Greene County in Mississippi on the same day. This also formed a squall line, hitting portions of Mississippi, Alabama, and Louisiana. Early afternoon on 5 March, a deadly EF2 tornado struck Rayne in Louisiana, killing a mother while she protected her daughter. At least twelve more people were injured. Initial evaluations indicated that sixty-two homes were destroyed and fifty more damaged. Additionally, two more EF0 tornadoes hit down in eastern North Carolina during this first week of March. Four days later, several tornadoes touched down from north Texas eastward to the Florida Panhandle, with Louisiana hit hardest. The most destructive EF2 tornado touched down just north of New Orleans.

Just near another fortnight later, a tornado developed in the afternoon of 21 March near Maxwell in California. It crossed Interstate 5 but did not cause any reported damage, as it was on the ground for only a few minutes. The same system produced more severe weather ahead of a dry line across eastern Nebraska, where tornadoes were reported northeast of Omaha. Later, a cluster of supercells began producing tornadoes in south central Iowa. A supercell is a thunderstorm that is characterized by the presence of a mesocyclone—a deep, continuously rotating updraft, sometimes also called rotating thunderstorms. They tend to be more severe and are often isolated from other thunderstorms but can dominate the local climate up to thirty-two kilometres away. Out of this supercell, a tornado was reported in Greenfield and later two more tornadoes near Winterset in Iowa. Several funnel clouds were seen in Des Moines with a possible touchdown. These funnel clouds were later associated with the storm that produced the first tornado to hit Greenfield and the following two in Winterset.

On 23 March, more tornadoes and severe weather developed, with the most significant tornadoes touching down in East Tennessee, where significant damage could be witnessed. Near Greenback in Blount County, an EF3 tornado was confirmed with rigorous damage in the area. Another EF2 notable tornado came down in southwestern Pennsylvania. Another week later, on 29 March, a warm front over the Gulf of Mexico associated with an upper-level low over Texas moved northward into the Gulf Coast states and brought scattered severe weather into the region. In neighbouring Louisiana, three tornadoes touched down, including an EF1 that caused a three-story building to collapse. In Mississippi, one person was killed after lightning caused a house fire. Also in Copiah County, a strong microburst took place and produced winds up to 180 kilometres per hour. This activity later shifted into central Florida on 30 March as a frontal boundary stalled out across the state. During the two-day period, altogether ten tornadoes touched down and a series of squall lines produced widespread wind damage on 31 March. The end of this month saw significant damage in several communities, with damage exceeding $5 million. Seven people got injured when one of the tornadoes hit a local festival.

If March was an active month, April would see even more tornado outbreaks. Several storms started to develop in the evening on 3 April. Storms in Kansas, Missouri, Iowa, and Illinois brought strong thunderstorms to the areas. A tornado watch was issued for Iowa and Illinois as the storms rolled through, and later, a severe thunderstorm watch for northeastern Illinois and southeastern Wisconsin was added. However, they did not develop into tornadoes. Continuing eastward, the system entered an environment factoring tornadic development, and two tornadoes could be reported in Kentucky during the early afternoon, both rated EF2 and resulting in injuries. As confirmed by local emergency services, a tornado near Hopkinsville caused significant damage to a manufacturing plant. Numerous buildings were destroyed, trapping residents within debris. In addition to the tornadoes, there was widespread wind damage as an extreme large squall line tracked across the southern United States, as over 1,400 severe weather reports were received by the Storm Prediction Centre, calculating wind gusts as high as 145 kilometres per hour across twenty states altogether. Those killed at least nine people, one of the deaths being a result of an EF2 tornado in Dodge County, Georgia. Power outages took place due to the extensive wind damage in numerous places. Nearly 100,000 to 147,000 residents reportedly lost power in Tennessee and Georgia, respectively.

The United States was not the only place to experience tornadoes. A very powerful tornado also struck seven districts in northern Bangladesh during the afternoon of 4 April. At least twelve people were reported killed and more than 150 injured as the tornado destroyed hundreds of homes and uprooted large swaths of vegetation.

Again, back in the US on 8 and 9 April a large storm system moved northward and eastward. While initial severe weather was limited, a lone supercell broke out ahead of a mesoscale convective system in Pulaski County, Virginia on the eastern end of the warm front the evening of 8 April. Two tornadoes were confirmed—one of which, a EF2, caused quite some damage in Pulaski. Numerous houses were damaged, and eight people were injured. During the afternoon hours of 9 April, supercells developed along the warm front and tracked through parts of Kentucky, Tennessee, and North Carolina, generating softball-sized hail and at least four tornadoes. During the evening hours of 9 April, severe thunderstorms also developed across Nebraska, South Dakota, and Iowa. A single supercell became tornadic over extreme western Iowa and produced a family of ten tornadoes over the course of five hours. The first was 1.21 kilometrs wide and struck Mapleton, Iowa. It destroyed about 100 homes. Due to a twenty-minute warning time, no fatalities took place and only fourteen to sixteen people became injured in the process. Officials blocked off the town, and Governor Branstad issued a disaster proclamation for the town. A day later, on 10 April, additional tornadic activity developed across Wisconsin, with several more tornadoes reported in this area.

Five days later, during the afternoon of 14 April, a possible significant tornado outbreak started setting up for eastern Oklahoma. Supercells explosively gained momentum over central Oklahoma. Several funnel clouds and two touchdowns were reported; however, these did not result in any damage. Several tornadoes were confirmed through storm chasers, but only one large, intense tornado caused severe damage in the towns Atoka and Tushka. Houses were destroyed and flattened. Needless to say, numerous injuries were reported. Twenty-five more people were injured in Tushka, and two people were killed.

In Arkansas, strong winds produced by thunderstorms killed at least seven people. It is unclear, though, if they were caused by tornadoes or straight line winds. During the late night hours into the morning of 15 April, tornadic activity lessened. However, by the late morning, supercell thunderstorms redeveloped over parts of Mississippi, and tornadoes began to touch down. For the northern Jackson metropolitan area, a tornado emergency had to be declared, as shortly after 11:00 a.m., a destructive tornado moved across with severe damage, possible injuries, and two reported fatalities. That afternoon, Mississippi State University spotters confirmed a large tornado in east central Mississippi and west central Alabama, and another tornado emergency had to be issued. This tornado was 1.2 kilometres in width. But all along, ninety tornado sightings were registered that day, and at least eight people died in Mississippi and Alabama in their path.

Two days later, on 16 April, another PDS tornado watch—along with a high-risk alert from the SPC—was issued for central and eastern North Carolina. At least twenty-four people died, and 135 were seriously injured. It was North Carolina's worst tornado outbreak in twenty-five years. Tornadoes also struck South Carolina, Virginia, Maryland, and Pennsylvania. Twelve of the North Carolina deaths took place in Bertie County. At the height of their outbreak, tornado emergencies were issued for Raleigh, Snow Hill, and Wilson. Twelve supercells produced at least twenty-five tornadoes in North Carolina, with at least thirty-two counties affected. A total of twenty-one businesses and 440 homes were destroyed; sixty-three of those homes were in Raleigh. About ninety-two businesses and 6,189 homes were destroyed significantly. 184 of those homes were in Raleigh.

Between 19 and 24 April, yet another severe weather event grew across the Midwest and southern Great Plains. Thunderstorms began in the late afternoon of the 19th, and in the early evening, large hail and several tornadoes developed. Considerable damage occurred near Bowling Green, Missouri and Girard, Illinois as a result of tornadoes; the latter one was rated EF3. Another large tornado was acting near Octavia, Oklahoma before the supercells merged into a very large squall line. Overnight, this line tracked eastward with widespread wind damage and many embedded tornadoes across several states. A few were as strong as EF2, but most were brief and weak. But in the early hours of 20 April, a tornado tore through a neighbourhood in Oregon, Ohio and left some significant damage in its path (but luckily no injuries). Three more tornadoes hit New Albany and Jeffersonville, Indiana. Both cities are just north of Louisville, Kentucky.

On 22 April, the outbreak continued, with several tornadoes causing damage in the Midwest—the most notable a violent EF4 which struck St. Louis, Missouri. It caused extensive damage to the region. A few more tornadoes were seen on 23 and 24 April; however, most did not cause any severe damages, though one EF2 caused structural damage in the town of Bardwell, Kentucky. Again on 22 April, severe weather developed across parts of the Midwest. The hardest hit area was the St. Louis metropolitan area. A destructive tornado tracked across the region, causing severe damage in several communities. Houses were destroyed in seven communities of this region. The Lambert St. Louis International Airport was hit hard and experienced severe damages to its numerous facilities. Not only were windows blown out of the terminals, but airplanes were also flipped in the field just like toys. The airport was initially closed to investigate damages but was partially reopened by the end of 23 April, whereas the heavily damaged Concourse C was to be closed indefinitely. This tornado was assessed as an EF4 based on findings of flattened houses in Bridgeton. But following assessments could establish that a single tornado tracked for 35 kilometres through parts of Missouri and Illinois. It reached a maximum width of 0.64 kilometres. Elsewhere, further tornadoes were seen, including an EF2 tracking through Henderson, Webster, and Union Counties.

The month of April had not seen the end yet in the United States. Between 25 and 28 April, another very historic tornado development now known as the 2011 Super Outbreak took place across much of the southern United States as well as parts of the Midwest and Northeast. This outbreak counted three hundred confirmed tornadoes, with 322 tornadic fatalities. It ranked as one of the worst in US history. More than three dozen tornadoes could be confirmed each day, with thirty-nine on 25 April, fifty-five on 26 April, a record 188 in just twenty-four hours on 27 April, and forty-five on 28 April. In terms of violent tornadoes, this event ranked third, with fourteen EF4-5 storms, behind the 1974 Super Outbreak and the 1965 Palm Sunday outbreak. The SPC issued a moderate risk of severe weather for three consecutive days centred over Arkansas through Tennessee.

By late afternoon of 25 April, several tornadoes already had been reported across a few states, including two which caused extreme damage in Oklahoma and Texas. Later, at 3:25 p.m., the SPC issued a PDS tornado watch for much of Arkansas and parts of Missouri, Oklahoma, Texas, and Louisiana. Tornadoes were scattered until early evening, when an intense tornado cell tracked near the Little Rock metropolitan region and a tornado emergency had to be declared for Vilonia, Arkansas. A 0.80 kilometre-wide EF2 tornado caused extensive damage through Vilonia, and at least four people died in the town, with many more injured.

On 27 April, a large tornado came down in Tuscaloosa, Alabama, killing at least forty-one people. The same catastrophic tornado hit the northern suburbs of Birmingham shortly thereafter. Birmingham television reporters, who were filming the tornado, said that even from miles away, the funnel was so wide that they could not zoom their cameras out far enough to get the entire funnel into the frame at once. On 28 April, The Weather Channel reported that the parent supercell of the Tuscaloosa and Birmingham tornadoes had also been responsible for a long string of tornadoes that first formed over Mississippi and persisted across Alabama, Georgia, and South Carolina before finally dissipating in southern North Carolina.

In an interview with Jim Cantore on The Weather Channel on 28 April, a Tuscaloosa resident said that the hospitals were full to the point of telling people not to go to them for simple broken bones, as there was no space or manpower left to treat non-life-threatening injuries. Cantore went further to say that this outbreak would rival that of the 1974 Super Outbreak; hence, he named it the Super Outbreak II. Between 27 and 28 April, over 180 tornadoes were registered. Over 305 deaths were reported as a result, with as many as 204 in Alabama alone.

The *Wall Street Journal* stated on 28 April, quote: "The death toll from a series of storms and tornadoes across the southern United States soared to 305 on Thursday, with 204 confirmed fatalities in the state of Alabama alone. "We have 204 for the state of Alabama, including 36 in Tuscaloosa," an emergency management spokeswoman said, referring to one of the worst-hit counties. Officials warned that the definitive toll of what was already the worst tornado disaster to hit the United States in decades would probably not be known for days. The overall toll includes 34 deaths in Tennessee, 33 in Mississippi, 14 in Georgia, 12 in Arkansas, five in Virginia, two in Missouri, and one in Kentucky, according to state officials." [*34]

President Obama approved Governor Robert Bentley's request on 27 April for emergency federal assistance, including search and rescue support. Though the National Weather Service had sent out people to survey the damage on 28 April, due to the large number of tornadoes across Alabama, the reports were not finalized for months to come. On 30 April, the death toll stood at more than 340 people across six states.

Hope that the tornadoes would reduce for the US during the following month of May proved to be of no avail. There were 370 tornadoes reported in May, of which 314 were confirmed for the United States.

In addition, one tornado each hit the Philippines and Taiwan. Both resulted in significant damage. One person was killed in Calumpit in Bulacan. On 10 May New Zealand awakened to the devastation of tornadoes. On 3 May, a line of showers and thunderstorms tracked into the Northland from the Tasman Sea and brought unsettled weather to much of the region. The New Zealand Met Service mentioned the possibility of strong thunderstorms being embedded within the line, producing small hail and gusty winds. Significant upward motion in the atmosphere could be seen developing in the area surrounding Auckland, which prompted the Met Service to issue a high risk of thunderstorms for this area. With low-level wind shear and helicity, the possibility of tornadic activity was only too present.

At 2:55 p.m. New Zealand time, a hook echo was apparent on the weather radar, which indicated strong rotation and a likelihood of tornado build up. Only several minutes later, around 3:00 p.m., a tornado struck the Auckland suburb of Albany. Winds of estimated 201 kilometres per hour caused this tornado to rank as a high-end EF2. It caused considerable damage all along a five-kilometre-long track in this region. Several cars were tossed up to 6.1 metres in the air by the storm, and pieces of iron roofing were seen ninety-one metres above the ground. A total of fifty homes sustained varying degrees of damage along the tornado's track. The most severe damage happened at a local shopping mall, where large portions of the roof were simply torn off. One person was killed, and at least twenty were injured. Damages from the storm were estimated to be in the tens of millions. New Zealanders, who are hardly accustomed to tornadoes, had a rather bitter awakening to Mother Nature's might. The Albany people now might get a sense of reality regarding what Americans have to go through most of the time.

Back in America, a strong upper-level ridge over the Mississippi River Valley produced a narrow axis of extreme instability from eastern Nebraska to central South Dakota on 9 May. In light of this, the SPC issued a slight risk of severe weather for much of South Dakota and Iowa as well as for parts of Minnesota, Missouri, and Nebraska. Wind shear in the region started to increase. This was enhanced by a mid-level jet and provided a more favourable environment for strong thunderstorms. During the course of the day, two tornados—an EF1 and an EF2—touched down in South Dakota. The stronger one of the two crumpled a transmission tower. Then, continuing into 10 May, the system slowly moved eastward, shifting the centre of more severe activity into the Upper Plains of Minnesota. With this, mainly large hail was produced measuring up to 6.4 centimetres in diameter on average. An EF1 tornado touched down as well, causing significant damage to a garage.

On 11 May, an upper-level low moved out of the four corner region into the Central Plains, prompting a moderate risk of hazardous weather from the SPC. The main threat from these storms was expected to be large hail. Later that day, the moderate risk was discontinued and replaced by a large area under a slight risk. According to the SPC, the issuance of a moderate risk was due to an "improper handling of ongoing storms." [*35] Tornadic activity has never been treated lightly in the United States, but human errors do occur. The tornadic activity during this specific event remained scattered and consisted only of short-lived events. In all, at least nine tornadoes and a few gustnadoes—specific types of short-lived, low-level, rotating clouds—touched down across four states. Most were in Nebraska and Iowa, and twin tornadoes of EF0 and EF1 struck the city of Lenox, damaging several homes. The weather moved eastward, and the low became diffuse, producing scattered severe weather on 12 and 13 May.

A week later, a small system of thunderstorms started to develop in Brown County, Kansas. At the same time—21 May—another system formed to the southeast of Emporia in Kansas. The Brown County system grew into a tornado over Shawnee County in Kansas and touched down over Topeka for several seconds, causing minor damage nearby. Meanwhile, the Emporia system moved to the northeast, where the EF3 tornado damaged the town of Reading heavily. One person was killed, and several others were injured. At least twenty houses were destroyed. After hitting Topeka, the tornado hit several towns, including Oskaloosa, Kansas, causing extensive damage to that community. Several other tornadoes touched down in the region that same evening.

For 22 May, a moderate risk of severe weather was announced for much of the Midwest south to Oklahoma. The first tornadic supercell that day developed during the mid-afternoon hours over the western Twin Cities with a swath of damage in and around Minneapolis, Minnesota. A very intense tornado also tracked towards Harmony, Minnesota that afternoon, and a tornado emergency was issued. Later, at about 5:15 p.m., a very large, intense, multiple vortex tornado resulted in catastrophic damage in Joplin,

Missouri. Many houses and businesses were flattened. Some were even blown away. The main hospital was heavily damaged, and many people were trapped in destroyed homes. The Weather Channel video showed entire communities flattened. Early reports suggested there were at least 125 fatalities, with the death toll rising later to at least 159, and another thousand were injured. This tornado was given a rating of EF5.

Two days later, in the late afternoon hours of 24 May, supercells began forming over western Kansas and Oklahoma. The National Weather Service predicted a dangerous tornado outbreak. As a line of powerful cells began to take shape, trained spotters reported large tornadoes near El Reno and in rural Grady County, Oklahoma. One of these, a rated EF5, swept from Binger to Guthrie and destroyed many homes, causing at least nine fatalities. It was the sixth of the year and the second of the outbreak sequence. Three other EF4 tornadoes developed among the many other tornadoes that day.

On 25 May, another EF3 tornado hit the city of Bedford, Indiana at around 10:00 p.m. US Route 50 was temporarily closed because of heavy debris. Another tornado touched down in Keyser, West Virginia and tracked as far as Berkeley Springs. A day later, strong thunderstorms travelled through the Cumberland Valley in South Central Pennsylvania. An EF1 tornado was witnessed near Carlisle, Mechanicsburg, and Hershey. Tornadoes also destroyed the setup for the Harrisburg Art festival scheduled to take place the following week. On 25 May, three tornadoes also hit the Sacramento Valley of California north of Sacramento. One tornado, an EF1 rating, struck east of Artois, uprooting hundreds of almond trees and causing damage to farm equipment and roofing materials. Another EF1 struck south of Durham, uprooting thousands of more almond trees, destroying an out building, and damaging a barn. An EF2-rated tornado struck northwest of Oroville and caused further heavy damage to a ranch and a garage.

Another four days later, a moderate risk of severe weather was ahead of the lower Great Lakes. Thunderstorm watchers were in place by late morning of 29 May as well as during the early afternoon hours for northern Illinois and a small portion of Indiana. In Iowa, a severe line of thunderstorms developed and tracked eastward. It produced scattered wind and hail over Illinois. But then a tornado watch was issued for southern Michigan, northern Indiana, and northern Ohio. As the storms crossed Lake Michigan, they weakened but then grew stronger again and began to exhibit rotation as they moved inland over southern Michigan, resulting in numerous tornado warnings. Kalamazoo, Battle Creek, Lansing, Jackson, Ann Arbor, and Flint were all warned. A funnel cloud and a possibility of a brief touchdown were reported in Vicksburg, and widespread wind damage fell on Battle Creek. An EF1 tornado tore roofs off of numerous buildings in Coldwater, and another EF1 was confirmed to have struck Shiawassee County near Perry.

With May gone, there were 177 more tornadoes reported in the United States for the month of June, of which at least ninety were confirmed. The Springfield tornado made most of the headlines. In the Northeast, thunderstorms began developing along the tail end of a cold front during the late morning hours of 1 June. By the early afternoon, a tornado watch was issued for parts of Connecticut, Massachusetts, Maine, New Hampshire, New Jersey, New York, Pennsylvania, and Rhode Island. A rare tornado outbreak for the Maine and Massachusetts began late that afternoon. Several tornadoes were confirmed. But during that afternoon, an EF3 tornado occurred in downtown Springfield, Massachusetts and several surrounding towns. Major damages were reported. There were some roofs that collapsed in downtown businesses. Damages to brick structures and numerous injuries were reported.

Significant damage also occurred in West Springfield, Monson, and other communities where houses were destroyed or even flattened. Three deaths have been attributed to the Springfield tornado thus far; it was the first killer tornado in Massachusetts since 1995. The Centre Plains later received a warning from the Storm Prediction Centre for a moderate risk of severe weather. By the evening hours, forty-eight tornadoes had touched down over rural areas. The next day, during the afternoon hours of 20 June, a PDS tornado watch went out for much of central Nebraska and north central Kansas. A significant threatening tornado could be expected. Additionally, very large hail at least ten centimetres in diameter was expected within this area. At around 1:00 p.m. local time, storm chasers saw a large EF3 tornado on the ground north of Hill City, Kansas and again later that afternoon near Elm Creek, Nebraska.

More and more tornadoes were reported across the region. Some were very large and intense, but luckily, most moved across open country. Warnings stretched from North Dakota to Kansas. Additional thunderstorm warnings went out for parts of Oklahoma and North Texas, as well. The 21st did not seem to slow the weather gods down. Tornado warnings were issued for several more areas, such as central Minnesota, Wisconsin, southern Illinois, parts of Missouri, and lower Michigan. Tornadoes were seen in Anoka County, Minnesota, Green Lake, and in the Fond du Lac Counties in Wisconsin. One major downfall happened in the Chicago Metropolitan area, with damage to much of Wheeling in Illinois. A series of tornadoes tracked across the Louisville, Kentucky area late on 22 June, with five tornadoes later confirmed in this area, including an EF2. One of the tornadoes directly hit Churchill Downs, severely damaging several buildings on the site. Other significant damage was witnessed in several industrial parks in the metropolitan area. Buildings were heavily damaged. New Zealand was again visited by two tornadoes in the city of New Plymouth, causing moderate damage.

For the month of July, tornado events slowed down a little for the United States. There were ninety-two tornadoes reported for July, of which at least thirty were confirmed. On 1 July, an extreme straight line wind and a derecho (right side) event took place over South Dakota, Minnesota, Wisconsin, and Iowa. Wind as high as 201 kilometres per hour caused extensive damage, especially along the border of Minnesota and Wisconsin. Furthermore, seven tornadoes touched down, out of which one was rated EF2.

During mid-July, numerous tornadoes touched down over the northern Plains on both 16 and 17 July at the edge of a very hot and humid air mass. At least sixty tornadoes (mostly in North Dakota) remained mainly over open country, but a few did cause significant damage. A house was destroyed by a strong EF3 in La Moure County.

The month of July also reported a tornado event in Alberta, Canada. At least four tornadoes touched down on various days, causing relatively minor damage. But twelve buildings over a one-block area were affected. Damaged roofs and flooded streets were reported.

In the whole of August, only fifty-two tornadoes were reported. At least twenty were confirmed. Early on 10 August, a strong EF2 tornado hit near Locust Grove, Oklahoma. This was more or less out of the blue, as tornadoes are a rarity in midsummer Oklahoma. It was embedded in a larger thunderstorm complex and destroyed a mobile home, killing one person and injuring two more. On 19 August, an isolated EF1-rated tornado with winds up to 169 kilometres per hour struck Wausaukee, Wisconsin and killed one person. Two days later, an intense tornado touched down late in the afternoon over Goderich, Ontario, severely damaging the downtown area with one strike. This was the strongest tornado in Ontario since 1996, and many buildings were damaged or destroyed. There had been earlier reports of two other tornadoes in the area. At least thirty-seven people were injured. A sixty-one-year-old worker at a salt mine was killed as winds of three hundred kilometres per hour raged. On the same day, Conquest, New York confirmed an EF2 tornado.

On 1 August, an F2 tornado struck the city of Blagoveshchensk, Russia. It remained on the ground for thirteen minutes, damaged over 100 homes and 150 cars, and uprooted 150 trees on its path. One person was killed, and twenty-eight received medical attention for injuries, with four hospitalized.

Between 26 and 28 August, Hurricane Irene made history. The outer bands and core of Hurricane Irene, which was reported to be a storm the size of Europe, produced numerous tornadoes as it made landfall first in North Carolina and then tracked further northward. Across several states along the immediate east coast of North America, several tornado reports came in. One tornado near Columbia, North Carolina was rated an EF2, caused severe destruction to several houses, and injured many. The East Coast remained on alert for more than thirty-six hours. The hurricane left extensive flood and wind damage along its path through the Caribbean and the East Coast of the US as far as Atlantic Canada. The ninth named storm and first major hurricane of that season, Irene formed from a well-defined Atlantic tropical wave that showed signs of organization east of the Lesser Antilles. It developed atmospheric convection and a closed cyclonic circulation centre, prompting the National Hurricane Centre to initiate public advisories on the tropical cyclone late on 20 August. Subsequent convective organization occurred as it passed the Leeward Islands, and by 21 August 21, it had moved very close to Saint Croix in the US Virgin Islands.

The next day, Irene made landfall at hurricane strength near earthquake-prone Puerto Rico, where high winds and intermittent torrents caused significant property damage. Irene tracked just north of Hispaniola as an intensifying Category 1 hurricane, skirting the coast with heavy precipitation and strong winds that killed several people. After having crossed the Turks and Caicos Islands, the hurricane strengthened into a Category 3 major hurricane while passing through the Bahamas. There it left behind a trail of massive structural damage in its wake. Curving towards the north, Irene skirted past Florida. Its outer bands produced tropical storm form winds. It made landfall over Eastern North Carolina's outer banks on the morning of 27 August and moved from there along southeastern Virginia, affecting the Hampton Roads region.

After briefly re-emerging over water, Irene mad a second US landfall near Little Egg Inlet, New Jersey the morning of 28 August. It was the first hurricane to make landfall in the state of New Jersey since 1903. Irene was eventually downgraded to a tropical storm as it made its third US landfall in the Coney Island area of Brooklyn in New York at approximately 9:00 a.m. local time. Eastern upstate New York and Vermont experienced most of the damage by Irene. Vermont suffered from the worst flooding in centuries. Through its path, Irene caused widespread destruction and at least forty-four deaths. Monetary losses in the Caribbean were as high as $3.1 billion (USD) according to preliminary estimates. Early damage estimates for the US are said to be about $7 billion.

Hurricane Irene was reported worldwide. I noticed how educational the reporting was done through news channels such as CNN, Fox, and even BBC. With that kind of educational information, everyone can learn to look at Mother Nature's events from different angles and become more prepared than ever before to protect himself or herself.

With Irene in the past, the next warning came with Tropical Storm Lee in early September. As of 4 September, fifteen tornadoes had already been reported in the US alone. None were confirmed, and this was only for the beginning of the month. The slow-moving storm Lee resulted in at least fourteen tornado reports along the immediate northern Gulf Coast beginning on 3 September and continuing into the 4th. My sister is living in this area, and I asked her to stay safe. She reported back to me on the 5th, saying it was bad and frightening, but all was good. Several areas of significant damage were reported from central Louisiana to the western Panhandle. Luckily, New Orleans stayed more or less unharmed. [*33]

I have purposely reported on Mother Nature's might rather thoroughly—specifically in regard to the events of the last twenty years. I believe it has become rather obvious that Mother Nature does deserve our respect in many ways. The year 2011 alone reminds us more and more how powerful our environment can be. It is a unique, beauty-and-the-beast package in its own rights. As magnificent our environment can be perceived, it can powerfully tell us of its might. And with more and more evidence, such disastrous events are now being explained not solely as Mother Nature's might, but also in connection with our planetary systems, and further away, with our universe.

Educating your children to respect nature is not just done with clearing up your favourite picnic spot and your holiday destinations alone, it seems. Mother Nature, our planetary systems, and the universe all deserve more respect than that. Part of an ongoing education with our children is to let them know of the powers Mother Nature and our extended environment can bring into one's neighbourhood. We can't protect our children by brushing tragic events under the carpet. Our children need to know. It's our means of respecting them. After all—and I repeat this—we as Homo sapiens are as much a part of the molecular chain within Mother Nature's existence as she is herself. Human beings carry their own unique beauty-and-the-beast package. While there are wonderful people around us, there are also less admirable species amongst us. They all still deserve respect as being within Mother Nature's or even universal existence, but we as human beings have the ability to choose how we give this respect to others. We can respect the wonderful ones and avoid contact with the less admirable ones. As much as we know where our shelters are when Mother Nature throws one of her wobbles, we must know how to shelter ourselves from people who do not deserve our respect. It is our choice. We don't need to develop suburbs in the pathways of tornado—or earthquake-prone regions. We don't need to build in areas known to floods. Neither do we need to erect nuclear power stations on fault lines known to us.

Within the awareness of our environment, I also would like to point out another beauty-and-the-beast package. It is the incredible science of microorganisms, bacteria, and viruses. As much as they seem to exist for the sake of equilibrium in a wider range than just the ecosystem, harmful danger lurks in this specific package—which brings us to the danger of epidemics. They can attack us and our environment in form of outbreaks of contractible diseases that spread at a rapid rate through animal and human populations alike. Some health disasters are called pandemics. They are the ones that spread globally, such as the Black Death, which was one of the most devastating pandemics in all human history.

One specific pandemic peaked in Europe between 1348 and 1350 and was for a long time thought to have been an outbreak of a plague caused by the bacterium *Yersinia pestis*. This assumption was challenged by a number of scholars from the 1970s but has been supported by genetic studies published since 2010. It apparently started in China and then travelled along the Silk Road and reached the Crimea (today's Ukraine) by 1346. From there, it is theorized that it carried Oriental rat fleas living on the black rats that had been regular passengers on merchant ships. Hence it spread throughout the Mediterranean and Europe and killed an estimated 30-60 percent of Europe's population. It was such a vital pandemic that it is estimated it reduced the world's population from an estimated 450 million to 350-375 million by 1400. The pandemic created a series of religious, social, and economic upheavals which had profound effects on the course of European history. It took 150 years for Europe's population to recover. The plague returned at various times, again killing more people, until it left Europe in the nineteenth century. [36]

I would like to repeat and draw awareness to the fact that bacteria and viruses again are part of the beauty-and-the-beast package of Mother Nature's (if not the universe's) existence. As much as bacteria and viruses are a tool for the body to strengthen the immune system, this very immune system can become defeated in the same process. Mother Nature works in miraculous ways.

During the last hundred years, significant pandemics have occurred. [37] In 1959, the AIDS pandemic made headlines; in 2002, the SARS pandemic; and during 2009 and 2010, the H1N1 influenza pandemic, better known as the swine flu. Other diseases spread more slowly but are nevertheless considered to be global health emergencies according to the

World Health Organization's assessment. The Ebola haemorrhagic fever has claimed hundreds of victims during several outbreaks in Africa, and malaria is killing an estimated 1.6 million people each year. The XDR-TB, a strain of tuberculosis, has become extensively resistant to drug treatments. It is obvious that we have to stay alert and not shy away from such pandemics and epidemics. They, too, deserve our utmost respect.

In modern times, famine has hit sub-Saharan Africa the hardest, although the number of victims of modern famines is smaller than the number of people killed by the Asian famines of the twentieth century. Still, famine is a subject that deserves attention. Alone during the last ten years, it has extensively hit the following countries. Between 2000 and 2009, the Zimbabwe food crises caused by Mugabe's land reform policies brought famine to the country, and in 2003, the Darfur conflict caused similar deprivation in Sudan's population. During 2005, both Malawi and Niger suffered through famine. In Niger, the famine continued into 2006. Additionally, Somalia, Djibouti, Ethiopia, and Kenya experienced the 2006 Horn of Africa food crisis. 2008 was devastating for all: China, North Korea, Somalia, Ethiopia, Kenya, Afghanistan, Bangladesh, East Africa, Tajikistan, Kenya, Sahel, and Somalia with the rest of its neighbouring countries. The cyclone Nargis devastated Burma's major rice-producing region, and ten million Kenyans are facing starvation.

Famine is a disaster. [*38] It is always accompanied or followed by malnutrition, starvation, epidemics, and increased mortality. It deserves looking at; in other words, it deserves respect. Emergency measures in relieving famine primarily aim to include providing deficient micronutrients, such as vitamins and minerals, through fortified sachet powders or directly through supplements. A famine relief model that is increasingly used by aid groups calls for giving cash or cash vouchers to the starving to pay local farmers instead of buying food from donor countries, as often required by law, as it wastes money on transport costs. But more importantly, it perpetuates the cycle of dependency on foreign imports rather than helping to create real local stability through agricultural abundance. Such independence, however, does rest upon local conditions of soil, water, temperature, and so on.

There are long-term measures in sight—for instance, investment in modern agriculture techniques, such as fertilizers and irrigation. These efforts are not as clear-cut, though, as the World Bank factors seem to restrict government subsidies for farmers. On the other hand, increasing use of fertilizers is opposed by some environmental groups because of its unintended consequences and adverse effects on water supplies and habitats. In other words, we all still have to learn a lot more before we can compete with Mother Nature's ability for equilibrium.

In this, we also have to warn our scientists within the pharmaceutical, health, and food industries to start acting cautiously. We have to ask them to *respicere*—to look back at—all the data collected by now and start to evaluate these data for what they are. These data are indicators of respect, not a power game of human species against nature. The new, evaluated respect is called human species with nature. The human species is not superior to nature's treasure chest; it's part of it, and let's not forget that.

If we look at our environment in these modern times, it seems it is expanding into the universe and space more and more. This is notably and in nearly the same ways asking to be looked at—to be respected, as Mother Nature has done for centuries now. Meteoroids have come down to earth with huge impacts in the past, but only now are we learning of such space disaster.

On 30 June, 1908, the media reported of the Tunguska meteoroid, which caused a powerful explosion near the Podkamennya Tunguska River in what is now known as Krasknoyarsk Krai in Russia. This explosion was reportedly originated by the air burst of a large meteorite or fragment of a comet at an altitude of five to ten kilometres above the earth's surface. Various studies have yielded different estimates of the object's size, with general agreement that it was a few tens of metres across. The number of scholarly publications on the predicament of the Tunguska explosion since its occurrence in 1908 may be estimated at about one thousand, mainly in Russia itself.

Although the meteoroid or comet burst in the air rather than hitting the surface, this event is still referred to as an impact. The energy of the blast assumingly ranged from five to as high as thirty megatons of TNT, with ten to fifteen megatons of TNT the most likely amount. Without getting too scientific about it, a TNT equivalent is a method of quantifying the energy released in explosions. The ton of TNT is a unit of energy equal to 4.184 gigajoules, which is approximately the amount of energy released in the detonation of one ton of TNT. The megaton, then, is a unit of energy equal to 4.184 petajoules. Anyway, the estimated ten to fifteen megatons would equal roughly the United States' Castle Bravo thermonuclear bomb tested on 1 March, 1954. In other words, this amount is about one thousand times more powerful than the atomic bomb dropped on Hiroshima in Japan and about one third the power of the Tsar Bomba, the largest nuclear weapon ever detonated.

The Tunguska explosion knocked over an estimated eighty million trees covering 2,150 square kilometres. The shock wave from the blast reportedly could have measured 5.0 on the Richter scale. [39] Needless to say, an explosion of this magnitude would be capable of destroying a large metropolitan area. Ever since this event, discussions regarding asteroid deflection strategies are ongoing.

Global satellite monitoring has only become possible since the 1960s and 1970s. Impacts of similar size of the Tunguska meteoroid before that would consequently have gone most likely unnoticed. But rest assured— they happened.

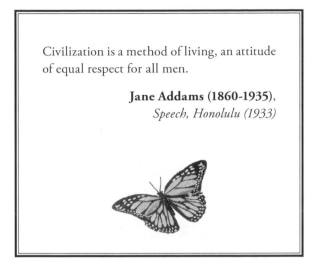

Civilization is a method of living, an attitude
of equal respect for all men.

Jane Addams (1860-1935),
Speech, Honolulu (1933)

RESPECT TOWARDS OUR SOLAR SYSTEM

Now to something that has made me curious for the last five or so years. New Zealand has very wet and cold winters, and the winter months drag out a bit. Its residents get tired of the winter by at least September and wish for the summer to come. We don't have autumn or spring seasons over here; instead, we go immediately from summer into winter and vice versa.

Some tourism brochures make believe that our spring time is from September through November, the summer from December to February, autumn from March to May, and winter from June to August. But truth be told, we experience no spring or autumn, as many do in Europe or the US. A summer as I know it from Europe I experience here in New Zealand from late October through February or mid-March. Then from April to September (lately, mid-October), it is winter. The winter months are moody like an April in Europe. Temperatures can differ up to 15⁰ C during night and daytime hours.

When I get up in the mornings during the winter months, the house is cold but soon warms up from the first sunrays, if we are lucky. And there is my curiosity. During the last five to six years, the sun has warmed the house a lot faster. The sun is hot, even during winter. Sometimes in winter, when the sun is out and heats my skin, I wonder how hot it will get during summer. It is sometimes already unbearable to stay in the sun for more than five minutes during winter. I have to admit that I am specifically sensible to temperature changes, but the fact still remains that the sun is getting hotter. I always wondered why.

Now the answer also comes from the universe in form of solar flares. A solar flare is a phenomenon where the sun suddenly releases a great amount of solar radiation—much more than normal. Once I heard about solar flares, I got very excited and looked into the matter of my curiosity.

The most powerful flare in the past five hundred years is believed to have occurred during September 1859. It also became known as the Solar Superstorm or the Carrington Event. Scientists state that it occurred during solar cycle 10 and remained the most powerful solar storm in recorded history. [*40] The history behind this is that ice cores contain thin, nitrate-rich layers that can be used to reconstruct a history of past events before reliable observations. These show evidence that events of this magnitude—as measured by high-energy proton radiation, not geomagnetic effect—do indeed occur approximately once every five hundred years, with events at least one fifth as large occurring several times per century. Less severe storms occurred back in 1921 and 1960, when widespread radio disruption also was reported. Back in 1859, from 28 August to 2 September, numerous sunspots and solar flares were observed on the sun. Just before noon on 1 September, the British astronomer Richard Carrington (hence the Carrington Event) observed the large flare, which caused a massive coronal mass ejection to travel directly towards earth, taking eighteen hours. This in itself was remarkable, because such a journey normally would take three to four days. But it had moved so quickly because an earlier coronal mass ejection had cleared its way.

On 1 September, Carrington and Richard Hodgson, another English amateur astronomer, independently made the first observations of a solar flare. Worldwide reports on the effects of the geomagnetic storm of 1859 were compiled and published by Elias Loomis. These reports support the observations of Carrington. Then, on 2 September, the largest recorded geomagnetic storm occurred. Auroras were seen around the world, most notably over the Caribbean. Also noteworthy were those over the Rocky Mountains that were so bright that their glow awoke gold miners, who began preparing breakfast because they thought it was already morning. According to Professor Daniel Baker of the University of Colorado's Laboratory for Atmospheric and Space Physics, "people in the northeastern US could read newspaper print just from the light of the aurora." [40]

Telegraph systems all over Europe and North America failed, in some cases even shocking telegraph operators. Telegraph pylons threw sparks, and telegraph paper spontaneously caught fire. Some telegraph systems appeared to continue to send and receive messages despite having been disconnected from their power supplies.

On 3 September, 1859, the *Baltimore American and Commercial Advertiser* reported, "Those who happened to be out late on Thursday night had an opportunity of witnessing another magnificent display of the aurora lights. The phenomenon was very similar to the display on Sunday night, though at times the light was, if possible, more brilliant, and the prismatic hues more varied and gorgeous. The light appeared to cover the whole firmament, apparently like a luminous cloud, through which the stars of the larger magnitude indistinctly shone. The light was greater than that of the moon at its full, but had an indescribable softness and delicacy that seemed to envelop everything upon which it rested. Between 12 and 1 o'clock, when the display was at its full brilliancy, the quiet streets of the city resting under this strange light, presented a beautiful as well as singular appearance." It is obvious that the observer back then witnessed a beauty-and-the-beast event of magnificent proportion. Just imagine such an event in our modern times controlled by electronic gadgets day in day out. Just imagine . . .

And then along came the X20 event on 16 August, 1989, which disrupted the power grids in Canada and was followed by a similar flare on 2 April, 2001. The latter was estimated as an X20 flare and was as strong as the record flare of August, 1989 according to Dr. Paal Brekke, the European Space Agency Deputy Project Scientist for the Solar and Heliospheric Observatory, one of a fleet of spacecraft monitoring solar activity and its effects on earth. The Monday flare and the August 1989 flare were the most powerful recorded since regular X-Ray data became available in 1976. Solar flares are among the solar system's mightiest eruptions. They are tremendous explosions in the atmosphere of the sun capable of releasing as much energy as a billion megatons of TNT. Caused by the sudden release of magnetic energy, in just a few seconds, flares can accelerate solar particles to very high velocities—almost to the speed of light—and heat solar material to tens of millions of degrees.

The flare erupted at 4:51 p.m. EDT Monday, 2 April, 2011, and produced an R4 radio blackout on the sunlit side of the Earth. An R4 blackout, rated by the NOAA SEC, is second to the most severe R5 classification. The classification measures the disruption in radio communications. X-ray and ultraviolet light from the flare changed the structure of the earth's electrically charged upper atmosphere (ionosphere). This affected radio communication frequencies that either pass through the ionosphere to satellites or are reflected by it to traverse the globe.

"We are perhaps lucky that this event didn't occur over the weekend, when the resulting CME would almost certainly have been aimed towards Earth," said Brekke. "A smaller flare-related CME event in March 1989 caused major power failures in Canada, and subsequent smaller events have disrupted communication and navigation satellites." [*41]

The most powerful flare ever recorded happened 4 November, 2003 and was measured to have been between X40 and X45. For most of us who are unacquainted with the magnitude of solar flares, it may be difficult to understand the extreme force of such an explosion. We might compare it with an earthquake of 15 on the Richter scale, but the two scales cannot be satisfactorily compared. This explosion, if transferred to the earthquake scale, would have been an earthquake of around 15 on the Richter scale. In other words, it was an out-of-category event the likes of which had never before been seen or experienced. Fortunately for our planet and its populace, most of the debris from the explosion was not entirely earth-directed. A glancing blow from the flare did bring displays of the Northern Lights several days later. Yet this is nothing compared to what would have happened if the flare had been targeted directly towards earth. What remains certain is that this particular solar explosion broke all records and was an event without precedence in living memory. [42]

Some may wonder if Mother Nature and the universe are still our friends or if they have become our enemies. The spate of extreme solar activity began towards the end of October 2003 with a series of massive solar eruptions. The largest of these measured X18 on the solar flare scale. A cluster of other X-flare explosions within a matter of days made this one of the greatest periods of solar activity on record. And yet again, this was nothing compared to the November explosion, which was the biggest and most violent event the solar system has produced within recorded memory. Of course, when learning about solar activities, I immediately questioned how this affects us. Is this why the sun seems so hot recently? But the precise effects of this solar bombardment are, in fact, hard to determine. The short-term aftermath usually could involve disruption of all forms of electronic communication with a severe threat to all space satellites and telecommunications, which we have come to be dependent on. Long-term effects are equally difficult to categorize, but it is believed that they could include highly disturbed weather patterns with a greater risk of earthquakes and volcanic eruption in those vulnerable locations. As times are proving, we did have some major volcanic eruptions recently.

We can't complain about earthquake events either; they are happening on a daily basis with increasing velocity. People on the South Island of New Zealand are still coping with the devastating February Christchurch earthquake, which disrupted Christchurch's flow of life, including the country's economic situation, in many ways.

More and more physical, emotional, and social consequences are being seen in the population that has been effected by eruptions of this nature. Some time ago according to the NASCA Website, a Russian study reportedly confirmed that solar eruptions do result in a greatly increased incidence of strokes and heart attacks. In 2007, I myself experienced three viral heart attacks in the course of just one year. Emotionally, the effects are of widely fluctuating feelings that at worst can result in broken relationships, despair, and depression. On a larger scale, research also clearly shows that solar activity has the potential to trigger general social unrest even to the point of inciting wars, riots, revolutions, and a deteriorating state of international harmony. I think we all can see the connection now by looking at Norway, the Arabian world, and the conflict between Muslims and Christians. But we also can see this at the alarming rising rate of crime and drug and alcohol abuse. Humankind, as well as nature, is experiencing unrest. Our molecular basis is most likely trying to achieve some form of equilibrium. But how will this be possible in a world full of humans whose only need seem to be to control, manipulate, and come out of it all as winners, as if we have declared war to the universe? I guess even an answer to this would be lost in the overwhelming confusion of it all.

The question has to be asked is this: can solar flares actually destroy all life on earth? Unfortunately, the answer is yes. Although the sun is said to be remarkably stable, it does go through phases of increased activity. I have become very interested in the subject of the sun due to all this and have hence recently subscribed to the NASA newsletter. I recommend that everybody who has the ability to go online subscribe to these newsletters. A fantastic array of information will come your way that you haven't even heard of before. NASA knows more than I ever imagined. We are currently exiting one such phase where solar activity was again at the peak of its eleven-year cycle. What was remarkable about the October 2003 event is that it sprung from a period when the sun was expected to be relatively calm. This shows how little we really know about the sun. Experts warn that lethal flare explosion could conceivably erupt at any moment in time. The fact that one has not done so for many thousands of years might be reassuring but does not offer comfort for long-term security. After all, Homo sapiens always has longed for security and safety. This longing however is contradicting the laws of existence and coexistence.

Perhaps the most sobering realisation of all is that there is absolutely nothing we could do stop such a flare. Humankind has been put in place within its own limitations. Sometimes it is, indeed, sobering when such realization happens. But the few of us who are extreme sensitive to our environment are also able at such times to sense the complexity of existence in its whole might. I often get a sense of being part of this existence, yet clearly of a very tiny size—like a sand corn at the beach or something even smaller. The most important realization in this has always been that I am, in fact, a part. I am not isolated or superior. And for me, this is where respect of the wholeness is due.

It is not at all necessary to call fear in when such realizations happen. Fear will only block our awareness of the here and now and subsequently will hamper all necessary actions for respect. Of course, fear also asks what causes solar flares. On a daily basis, we have become accustomed to ask why. Mothers all over the globe tear their hair off their heads when their little ones go on and on all day with just one question: "Why?" I have always been more interested how things are happening. I like to know the process of an occasion rather than the reason.

In regard to solar flares, we still have a lot to learn, but from NASCA research, we can learn now that major solar flares are supposedly directly linked to still other celestial phenomenon, such as planetary alignments. With such understanding, the limits of our planetary environment start to expand even further and become nearly borderless. For instance, this current spate of solar activity occurred at a time when the sun was ringed with aligned planets. To NASCA, this is not a coincidence, and it is their belief that once these aligning planets disperse to less influential positions, then solar activity will once again return to normal levels. Yes, the risk remains that perhaps one day, an alignment will arise capable of triggering a solar Armageddon against which we shall have no defence at all. Well, if we ever needed a wakeup call to our very vulnerable position in the universe, then the sun has well and truly delivered it.

Reportedly since 4 November, 2005, the solar activity has returned to more normal levels. However, if there is one thing we can be certain about in regards to the sun, it is that nothing is definite. Its periods of fiery activity alternate between well-balanced periods of calm are temptingly comforting. However, one mere fact remains reality—that for all the many great years of study, we human beings still have no idea what the sun may do next. One thing, though, we know and teach our children is this: Never look at the sun directly, as this can cause permanent damage to your eyesight.

So does our solar system deserve our respect? Does he—*el sol,* the sun god—needs looking at, or *respecere?* Or is it respectful to simply recognize his existence with all the glory and the fury the sun god sends to our planet? Just remember how much we rely on him for our well-being. The sunlight is earth's primary source of light. Our existence and the existence of nearly all life on earth are fuelled by light from the sun. Our bodies produce vitamin D from sunlight. A lack of sunlight is considered one of the main causes of seasonal affective disorders, a serious form of the winter blues.

In this context, I also would like to quickly mention gamma ray bursts, which are the most powerful explosions that occur in our universe. [*43] These release an enormous amount of energy in just milliseconds or lasting for ten seconds. They release the same energy that the sun would have given in its entire life or even more than that. Though you might not have heard of them on a daily basis, they are in fact not rare at all, because they do occur about once every day and are detected by telescopes both on earth and in space. Most large masses of stars bigger than the sun can produce a so-called GRB. A GRB of distances nearer than eight thousand light years may cause a concern to life on planet Earth. Mainly Wolf Rayet stars WR104 can produce such GRB. Those Wolf Rayet stars are often referred to as WR stars and are evolved, massive stars which are losing mass rapidly by means of a very strong stellar wind with speeds up to two thousand kilometres per second. While our sun, as an example, loses approximately 10^{-14} solar masses every year, the WR stars typically lose 10^{-5} solar masses a year. WR stars are, needless to say, very hot. They have surface temperatures in the range of 25,000-50,000 K. The measurement K is a measurement unit for temperature defined by the Glasgow University engineer and physicist William Thomson, 1st Baron Kelvin who wrote of the need for an absolute thermometric scale, the Kelvin scale. Unlike the Fahrenheit and Celsius degrees, the Kelvin is not referred to or typeset as a degree. The Kelvin is the primary unit of measurement in the physical sciences, but is often used in conjunction with the Celsius degree, which has the same magnitude: absolute zero at 0 K is–273.15 °C (–459.67 °F). [44]

Astronomers with today's knowledge believe that the Ordovician-Silurian extinction—the second most destructive extinction on earth—might have been due to a GRB.

But don't be too alarmed. This extinction occurred 443.7 million years ago during one of the most significant diversifications in earth's history. It also marked the boundary between the Ordovician and following Silurian period. During this extinction event, there were several marked changes in biologically responsive carbon and oxygen isotopes. And this complexity may indicate several distinct, spaced events or particular phases within one event. Interestingly enough, at that time, most complex multi-cellular organisms lived in the sea, and around 100 marine families became distinct, covering about 49 percent of faunal genera. The brachiopods and bryozoans were decimated, along with many of the trilobite, conodont, and graptolite families.

I'd like to finish this chapter by leaving noteworthy information in regard to our environment. In November 2007, Reuters reported that weather-related disasters have quadrupled over the last two decades according to a leading British charity. From an average of 120 disasters a year in the early 1980s, there were now as many as five hundred, with Oxfam attributing the rise to unpredictable weather conditions caused by global warming. Barbara Stocking, the Oxfam Director, stated, "This year we have seen floods in South Asia, across the breadth of Africa and Mexico that have affected more than 250 million people." *45

This statement was four years ago on 25 November, 2007. Barbara also said, "This is no freak year. It follows a pattern of more frequent, more erratic, more unpredictable, and more extreme weather events that are affecting more and more people. The number of people affected by disasters has increased by 68 percent from an average of 174 million a year between 1985 and 1994 to 254 million people a year between 1995 and 2004. Action is needed," she insisted. "We now need to prepare for more disasters, otherwise humanitarian assistance will be overwhelmed, and recent advances in human development will go into reverse."

Oxfam wanted the UN conference on Climate Change in Bali in December 2007 to agree on a mandate to negotiate a global deal to provide assistance to developing countries to cope with the impacts of climate change and reduce greenhouse gas emissions.

Incidentally, Oxfam is an international confederation of fifteen organizations working in ninety-eight countries worldwide to find lasting solutions to poverty and injustice. Oxfam works directly with communities and seeks to influence the powerful to ensure that poor people can improve their lives and livelihoods and have a say in decisions that affect them. Originally, Oxfam was founded in 1942 in Oxford as the Oxford Committee for Famine Relief by a group of Quakers, social activists, and Oxford academics. Now this has changed into Oxfam Great Britain and still is based in Oxford. Their mission was to persuade the British government to allow food relief through the Allied blockade for the starving citizens of Axis-occupied Greece. The first overseas Oxfam was founded in 1963 in Canada. The organization changed its name to its telegraph address, OXFAM, in 1965.

The figures of OXFAM are alarming, yes. Yet the slight sense of respect before nature creeps up in my body, knocking on my own door of consciousness, saying that nature will have its way. It always had, and it always will. As long as I have this sense of being a tiny molecular part of existence, I will remain respectful of this process.

> It is a fine thing to establish one's own religion
> in one's heart, not to be dependent on tradition
> and second-hand ideals. Life will seem to you,
> later, not a lesser, but a greater thing.
>
> **D. H. Lawrence (1885-1930)**

RESPECT TOWARDS CULTURAL BELIEFS

Religion is basically a collection of cultural systems, belief systems, and worldviews that institutes symbols which then communicate spirituality and moral values to humanity. Consequently, many religions have narratives, symbols, traditions, and sacred histories which are intended to give meaning to lives or even to explain the origin of life, including the origin of the universe. In this, religions tend to acquire morality, ethics, religious laws, or a preferred lifestyle from their ideas about the cosmos and human nature.

Often, though, the word "religion" is used interchangeably with "faith" or "belief system," but religion commonly differs from private belief in that it has a much greater public aspect. Most religions show organized behaviours and clerical hierarchies; a definition of what constitutes devotion or membership; people attending worship, regular meetings, or services for the purpose of respect of a deity or for prayer; holy places; or scriptures.

In this I might again ask for caution by asking if the respect of a deity is superior to respect of mere existence.

Obviously, the development of religion has taken different forms in different cultures. Whereas some religions place an emphasis on belief, others place their accent on practice. Some focus on a subjective experience of a religious individual; others consider the activities of their religious community to be the most important. There are even religions that claim to be universal, believing their laws and cosmology to be binding for everyone, while others are intended to be practiced only by a closely defined or localized group. It is of no surprise that religion in many places has been associated with public institutions such as education, hospitals, the family, government, and yes, also the political hierarchies.

As we look at the term "religion" and its origin, we can learn from the Latin language that it derived from the term "*religionem.*" Translated into English, this means "respect for what is sacred, reverence for the gods." The bond between man and the gods was derived from the Latin word "*religio*"—"faithfulness" or "conscientiousness." Over time, from Cicero to Lactantius and from modern scholars such as Tom Harpur or Joseph Campbell, the origin of the world "religion" assumed many other derivations, mostly from the Latin verb "*religare*"—"to bind, to tie." It was mainly Cicero who extended the verb *religo* to a meaning of conscientiousness. At this point in history, it is said that many other cultures around the world, including Egypt, Persia, and India have a similar power structure and what today is called ancient, they would have only called law. During medieval times, religion became order—a bonded community, such as a monastic order. This eventuated in an independent source of power within the societies of their time. In some religions, like the Abraham religions, it is still today held that most of the core beliefs have been divinely revealed.

Only during the nineteenth and twentieth centuries did the academic practice of comparative relation divide religious belief into philosophically defined categories—the so-called world religions. A current state of psychological study about the nature of religiousness suggests that it is better to refer to religion as a largely invariant phenomenon that should be distinguished from cultural norms.

The four largest religious groups by population estimated to account for more than six billion people are Christianity, Islam, Buddhism, and Hinduism. In this, Christianity contains up to 32 percent, Islam up to 26 percent, Buddhism up to seven percent, and Hinduism up to 14 percent of the world's population. [46]

The oldest Abrahamic religions have reportedly all descended from Abraham and are what we call monotheistic religions, meaning the belief in just one God. These include Judaism and Christianity, including the Catholic Church, Protestantism, and Eastern Christianity. There are smaller groups still, such as Jehovah's Witnesses or the Latter-Day Saint movement, whose inclusion in Christianity sometimes becomes disputed.

Muslims all pray around Kaaba, the most sacred site in Islam. Islam is taught by the Islamic prophet Muhammad, an important political and religious figure of the seventh century. Islam is the dominant religion of northern Africa, the Middle East, and South Asia. As with Christianity, there is no single orthodoxy in Islam but a multitude of traditions which are generally categorized as Sunni and Shia, although there are other minor groups as well. Another Muslim group, the Bahá'í faith, was founded in the nineteenth century in Iran and since then has spread worldwide, teaching unity of all religious philosophies. The Bahá'í Faith accepts all of the prophets of Judaism, Christianity, and Islam.

There are smaller regional Abrahamic groups still, such as the Samaritans, who are primarily found in Israel and the West bank; the Rastafari movement in Jamaica; and the Druze in Syria and Lebanon.

With this, we have not yet touched on the variety of Indian religions, of which mainly Hinduism, Jainism, Sikhism, and Buddhism are foremost known. There are dozens of new religious movements within Indian religions and Hindu reform movements, such as Ayyavazhi or Swaminarayan faith. Iranian religions are also very ancient religions whose roots predate the Islamization of the greater Iran nowadays such as Zoroastrianism, Mandaeism, and Kurdish religions.

At this stage, I also would like to draw attention to all the folk religions, a term applied loosely to less-organized practices like those of paganism, shamanism, ancestor worship, or totemism all found in African traditional religions, in the religions of the Americas, in the Aboriginal culture of Australia, and in the Chinese, Korean, and Japanese religions.

In today's world, critics of religious systems as well as of personal faith have posed a variety of arguments against religion. Some modern-day critics hold that religion lacks effectiveness in human society; they may regard religion as irrational. Some assert that dogmatic religions are morally deficient, elevating as they do to moral status ancient, illogical, and ill-informed rules. We hear of atheists—those who lack the belief in any gods—or of irreligious movements in which an absence of any religion is promoted.

Some Mayo Clinic researchers, though, have examined the association between religious involvement and spirituality and physical health, mental health, health-related quality of life, and other health outcomes. The authors reported that most studies show that religious involvement and spirituality are associated with better health outcomes, including longevity, coping skills, and health-related quality of life and less anxiety, depression, and suicide.

The biggest argument against religion, without any doubt, comes from the many religious scenes of violence over the centuries. We only have to go back to the Crusades—the purely military campaigns between

Christian Europe and the Muslims. The argument that religions claim divine favour for themselves over and against other groups supports the tendency that this sense of righteousness would lead to violence. Critics of religion go even further and argue that religions do tremendous harm to society by using violence to promote their goals. One might argue that all monotheistic religions are inherently violent because of elitism that inevitably fosters violence against those who are considered outsiders. This simply leads to the question: Does religion in its own right deserve respect? I think we have to again differentiate between individuality and religious pluralism. The faithful individual deserves respect because of his or her mere existence. A proclaimed public authority of a religion, however, again remains anonymous and cannot be looked at—cannot be the object of *respecere*. The use of violence in this field is more an expression of this proclaimed public authority of religion than an expression of its individuality.

When religions become a purely military campaign, then we cannot speak of respect any longer. "You shall not kill" is the fifth commandment of the Catechism of the Catholic Church, but in political campaigns, killing—respectively, harming others—becomes the foremost goal.

Since the 9/11 events in New York, the word *"jihad"* has been more used than ever before. *Jihad* is the Islamic term for a religious duty of Muslims. In the Arabic language, the term *"jihad"* translates as a noun meaning "struggle." It appears forty-one times in the Quran and frequently in the idiomatic expression "striving in the way of God." A person engaged in *jihad* is called a *Mujahid*. Although *jihad* is an important religious duty for Muslims (some may refer to this as the sixth pillar of Islam), independently, it actually occupies no such official status. Traditionally, *jihad* was understood to be purely a military effort. In an offensive war, it is an obligation on the Muslim community as a whole; in a defensive war, sadly, it becomes a personal obligation on every adult male Muslim within the context of compliant respect. The war was primarily considered to be against unbelievers—those not of the Islamic faith. Other interpretations by reformers and modernizers in the nineteenth and twentieth century argue that *jihad* is primarily a moral and spiritual struggle. But in Western societies, the term *jihad* has, over time, mainly been translated by Muslims as "holy war." Scholars of Islamic studies often stress that these words are not synonymous. Muslim authors, in particular, tend to reject such an approach and stress non-militant connotations of the word.

Whatever *jihad* might be, the fact is that New York again is beefing up security ahead of its tenth anniversary of September 11 in 2011. It is reported that the lower Manhattan force will eventually rise to 670 members larger than any of the seventy-six precincts in the five boroughs and entire police departments in other cities across the country. The thousands of people expected to visit the September 11 memorial after it opens in the fall of 2011 will endure airport-style screening and be watched by closed-circuit cameras within all logistic public terminals as part of the attack site opens publicly for the first time since the 2001 terror attacks. Securing the World Trade Center site (which also has a skyscraper rising above the skyline) from terror attacks has been one of law enforcement's most pressing problems long before the al-Qaida attack that destroyed the towers. [*47]

In 1993, Islamic extremists exploded a rental van rigged with a fertilizer bomb in a Trade Centre parking garage, killing six people and injured more than one thousand others. In 2006, authorities alleged that a Lebanese man loyal to Osama bin Laden plotted to flood the site and the rest of lower Manhattan by exploding backpacks in commuter train tunnels under the Hudson River. While some view the resurrection of the 6.5 hectare property as a triumph of the nation's resolve, law enforcement believes terrorists see it as just another chance to prove their tenacity. "Without question it is a target, because it has tremendous symbolism," said James Kallstrom, a former top FBI official. The site isn't the target of a current known plot, but it "remains squarely in the terrorists' crosshairs," believes police commissioner Raymond Kelly of New York. Fears of a repeated plot against the site years ago resulted in its signature skyscraper being redesigned.

An original plan putting one World Trade Centre 7.6 metres off a state highway near the Hudson River had raised concerns by the NYPD that it could be vulnerable to car or truck bombs. A redesign moved it farther off the street and incorporated a windowless sixty-metre base. Developers and law enforcement have grappled with how to best police the anticipated steady flow of tourists, workers, and commerce at the site without necessarily turning it into an inhospitable armed camp. The top counterterrorism adviser to the former Governor George Pataki in mid-2002 was the architect of an ambitious security plan for the One World Trade Centre, which was scheduled to open in 2012. The National September 11 Memorial and Museum and other office towers and transit were to be at the site. Combining architectural innovation, high-tech gadgetry, and good old-fashioned manpower all provided by the NYPD, the Port Authority of New York and New Jersey police, including private security firms, would make it a very secure site.

Police are also planning to use a vehicle security centre to screen tour buses, trucks, and cars before they enter the site and park. Deliveries are planned through an underground roadway, and pedestrian traffic, including visitors to the museum, will be screened before entering the central plaza. Ticketed visitors to the memorial will be funnelled into a security screening room with airport-style metal detectors and X-ray machines. Employees and frequent visitors will be pre-screened so they can bypass regular checkpoints.

The security plan also calls for four hundred closed-circuit surveillance cameras in and around the Trade Center site. Live feeds will be monitored around the clock at an NYPD command centre located in a private office building near Wall Street. A computer system there uses video analytic computer software designed to detect potential threats (like unattended bags) and retrieve stored images based on descriptions of terror or other criminal suspects. Final touches are also being put on another ambitious piece of the plan: screening every car, truck, and other vehicle for radioactive materials that are evidence of a possible dirty bomb and other potential threats as they enter lower Manhattan. To achieve that, police are installing cameras, radiation detectors, and license plate readers at the sixteen bridges and four tunnels going in and out of Manhattan. In addition to New York police, Port Authority of New York and New Jersey police officers are also on the site; the agency wouldn't disclose how many for security reasons.

In all, the *jihad* as the Western world has come to know it is far from preaching peace and love, let alone respect. The world—not only New York and America—is living in fear of when the next terrorist attack is going to strike.

Fear certainly is not a good motivator for the modality of respect. If we all only can look at or *respicere* fear, then one thing becomes clear: Respect has gone, and fear has come.

With that fear comes a sobering $3.7 trillion (USD) to the USA's national debt for war and homeland security spending. At least 236,500 people have been killed, most of them civilians. The Costs of War study by the Watson Institute for International Studies at Brown University in Rhode Island indeed shows serious figures resulting from the September 11 attacks. The study was first published in June 2011 and was updated only recently on 4 September with new death toll estimates based on data from the first half of the year 2011. The dollar figures remained unchanged from June. According to these data, the September 11 attacks themselves killed 2,995 people and caused an estimated $50-100 billion (USD) in economic damage. The financial toll is as follows: [*48]

Tasks	US Dollar Amount
Congressional war appropriations to Pentagon since 2001	$1.3 trillion
Additions to Pentagon base budget	$362-652 billion
Interest on Pentagon war appropriation	$185 billion
Veterans' medical claims and disability	$33 billion
War-related international aid	$74 billion
Additions to Homeland Security base spending	$401 billion
Projected obligations for veterans care to 2050	$589-934 billion
Social costs to veterans and military families to date	$295-400 billion
Future spending requests outlined as follows:	
2012 Pentagon war spending	$118 billion
2012 foreign aid	$12 billion
2013-2015 projected war spending	$168 billion
2016-2020 projected war spending	$155 billion
ESTIMATED TOTAL	$3.7-4.4 trillion
With additional interest payments to 2020	$1 trillion
DEATH TOLL	**Figures**
Total low estimate	236,500
Total high estimate	261,700

DEATH TOLL ESTIMATES BY WAR ZONE			
Afghanistan	**Iraq**	**Pakistan**	**Yemen**
30,400-45,600	171,000	35,000-45,000	105

DEATH TOLL ESTIMATES BY CATEGORY					
US military	**US contractors**	**Other allied troops**	**Iraqi civilians**	**Iraqi security forces**	**Iraqi army during US invasion**
6,226	2,300	1,192	126,000	10,100	10,000
4,477 Iraq					
1,749 Afghanistan					
Iraqi insurgents	**Afghan civilians**	**Afghan security forces**	**Afghan insurgents**	**Journalists and media workers**	**Humanitarian workers**
19,000	12,423-14,701	5,138-8,000	10,000-20,000	170	279

One needs to ask: For the sake of achieving pluralistic societies, do those figures justify their aims? Do they even in the slightest, in fact, satisfy pluralistic needs?

Today, some US politicians argue that the Iraq war has at least made most Arabian countries aware of what they had to deal with under dictatorships and despot governments. The Arabian nations now strongly call for democracy; their rebellion against anything under a past dictatorship would make the September 11 losses along with the losses from the Iraq war more reasonable. The Arab Spring is the name of the revolutionary wave of demonstrations and protests occurring in the Arab world since December 2010. Revolutions are happening everywhere—Tunisia; Egypt; a civil war in Lybia; civil uprising in Bahrain, Syria, and Yemen; major protests in Algeria as well as in Iraq, Jordan, Morocco, and Oman; and further minor protests in Kuwait, Lebanon, Mauritania, Saudi Arabia, the Sudan, and Western Sahara. Clashes at the borders of Israel in May 2011 also have been inspired by the regional Arab Spring.

One has to ask again whether a call for either *jihad* or democracy justifies the death of thousands. And furthermore, isn't the wish for democracy just an umbrella name for creating even further pluralistic economic societies in which even more people will lose their identity and individuality for the sake of a the god of money? We must also not forget that the war industry plays a huge part in a pluralistic economic society,

Will the god of money in the end unite the world and bring back respect, belonging, or peace? Personally, I have my doubts. I have witnessed over the last years how respect towards any living matter—nature, micro-organisms, fauna, flora, and human beings alike—has eventually lost its homeland and its grounds to flourish on.

In this connection, I also would like to look at the recent July-August 2011 events in Norway. A thirty-two-year-old man accused of a massacre at a youth camp in Norway and a bombing in the capital, Oslo, has admitted responsibility for his actions, which he described as "gruesome but necessary." At least eighty-five people died when this gunman ran amok on Utoeya Island on Friday 22 July, hours after an Oslo bomb already had killed seven people. As Norway mourned the victims, police continued to search for the missing. At least four people from the island camp shooting have yet to be found. It is thought some may have drowned after swimming out into the lake to escape the hail of bullets. Police have been using a miniature submarine to search for the missing bodies. The police in Oslo said the death toll could rise further, as bodies or body parts were in buildings damaged by the bomb that are still too unstable to search. Police have also said another person may have been involved in that Friday's attacks, which happened within hours of each other.

The main suspect thought it was gruesome having to commit these acts, but in his head, they were necessary. This was revealed by the man to his lawyer. Reportedly, the man had planned these attacks for some time. The suspect has meanwhile been charged with committing acts of terrorism and is due to appear in court in the coming week in late July. Judges need to decide whether he should be detained as the investigations continue. It is believed that the suspect had links with right-wing extremists. Pictures of him wearing a wetsuit and carrying an automatic weapon appeared in a twelve-minute anti-Muslim video called "Knights Templar 2083" which appeared briefly on YouTube.

People in Oslo were speechless after these attacks. In heavy rain, with the sound of thunder in the air, people stood in a circle outside Oslo's cathedral. In the middle of the circle was laid a carpet of flowers illuminated by candles. People hugged, held hands, and stood in silence and in complete loss of understanding. Eyes were bloodshot from crying. Tears were dripping down from many faces. One Norwegian man said, "It feels like living on the outskirts of fear." It has been revealed that the thirty-two-year-old suspect had planned his attacks for years.

His planning was fed by his views on multiculturalism and Muslim immigration. He claimed to be a follower of the Knights Templar, a medieval Christian organisation involved in the Crusades and sometimes worshipped by white supremacists. Police have not speculated on motives for the attacks, but the Oslo bomb targeted buildings connected to Norway's governing Labour Party, and the youth camp on Utoeya Island was also run by the party.

The suspect's online documentations referenced to targeting "cultural Marxists/ multiculturalists traitors." Norway had problems in the past with neo-Nazi groups, but the assumption was that such groups had been largely eliminated and did not pose any significant threat any longer according BBC's speaker Richard Galpin.

Amongst the mourners in Norway were also Muslims who were making their way into the church to pay their respect. Many of them initially thought the bomb was the work of al Qaeda. Even Muslims in Norway agree that they live in a country that accepts everyone. Norway welcomes everyone. Residents had to realize it was a Norwegian himself who was responsible for such atrocity.

More and more details about the suspect came to the forefront. This young terrorist described himself as a Christian and conservatives on public Internet pages attributed to him. He grew up in Oslo and attended a School of Management. He had set up a farm, which enabled him to buy fertilizer, which may have been used to make a bomb. He was reported to have been armed with two weapons, one of them an automatic rifle. Whilst he openly expressed his views online, there was little to indicate that this young man—described by friends as quiet, friendly, and ordinary—would go on to kill dozens of people, many in cold blood.

But the very young man was seen by eyewitnesses on the island on the day of the attacks as a completely different person. It was a horrifying picture of events, these witnesses recalled—a blond man dressed as a policeman asking people to gather round and then opening fire at random. While some were shot as they tried to swim to safety, others cowered in undergrowth, hid in buildings, or pretended to be dead amid the bodies of other victims. The gunman simply continued his rampage.

This quiet, friendly, and ordinary-seeming young man reportedly had no military background except for ordinary national service. He had no criminal record. When police demanded that he put down the weapon, he did so—but by then, his shooting spree had already lasted ninety minutes.

Yet this quiet, friendly, and ordinary-seeming young man was not that unknown to the wider public. On the Facebook page attributed to him, he described himself as a Christian and a conservative. His interests included bodybuilding and freemasonry. A Twitter account attributed to the suspect has also emerged, but it only had one post, which was a quote from philosopher John Stuart Mill: "One person with a belief is equal to the force of 100,000 who have only interests."

Reportedly, both social networking sites were set up just days before the events of 17 July, when this young man's paranoia about the Islamization of Western Europe and the perceived failure of his country's political leadership to stop its advance at home grew.

The same very quiet and friendly young man was also a member of a Swedish neo-Nazi internet forum called Nordisk, and he had formulated an absolute policy of hatred of anything that was non-Nordic. He was looking at planning how to take over the world in a rather insane, over-complicated, deluded manner.

Hitler comes to mind. This young man portrayed himself as equally meticulous in his development of his philosophy as well as in his research. To the court, he appealed that he was trying to "save Norway and Western Europe from cultural Marxism and a Muslim takeover." Even though he admitted to carrying out the attacks in July, he did not plead guilty to charges of terrorism. The accused explained to the court that the Labour Party had failed the country and the people, and the price of their treason was what they had to pay.

I mentioned the analogy to Hitler before. What strikes me most is that this young man was born nearly thirty-five years after the end of the Holocaust and WWII. Another thirty-two years later, the shadow from the past hits back again.

In the name of religion, beliefs, and cultural belonging, are we learning anything, or are we just repeating history over and again? Respect, it seems, does not go along with religion, beliefs, and cultural belonging. These are still too closely connected to a still-superior mind of Homo sapiens! Isn't it time to look back at our real essence of origin, no matter what religion, faith, or cultural belonging we have been brought up in? These are, after all, just a mere periphery of a temporary existence on planet Earth. Our essence of origin goes far beyond this periphery.

> Go confidently in the direction of your dreams! Live the life You've imagined. As you simplify your life, the laws of the universe will be simpler.
>
> **Henry David Thoreau (1817-1862)**

RESPECT TOWARDS OURSELVES

Years ago, I was told a parable. I cannot recall who wrote this story. It was just told amongst my friends in the late 70s or early 80s.

Once upon a time, each baby born received a pillow from a friendly little elf. The pillow was given to the mother prior to birth to comfort the baby—to let the baby know that this pillow would be there for him or her forever. Even if Mum had to go to the toilet, do the dishes, go shopping, talk on the phone, entertain visitors, etc., this pillow always would be there, like a friend. If Mum could not be hugged, this pillow could. But there was an old, embittered witch living in the neighbourhood who got really envious of these pillows, as no one ever had given her a pillow, let alone when she was a baby.

The witch thought, *I could build a factory and make nice, new, shiny pillows—nicer than the ones the elf is giving away.* So the witch launched her Hug-Me Pillow Factory and started producing. Everybody thought this was a wonderful idea, and people started buying Hug-Me pillows, one after another. The buyers would sit alone at home and hug their wonderful purchases. If they got tired of the one pillow they had, they bought another one—a bigger, shinier, more expensive one. The factory went well, and the witch earned more than she had bargained for. She started opening factories in other countries and became world-renowned for her pillows. After all, everybody wanted a hug—oops, I mean a pillow! The demand for her pillows would never cease; the witch knew this.

The little elf still rushed into the homes of mothers-to-be to give them their pillows for the event to come, but most of these young mothers by now already had pillows from the Hug-Me Pillow Factory and declined the elf's pillows. Sadly, the elf left one home after another without being able to leave her pillow behind for the precious newborns.

And so times changed. Appearances, values, pricing, and size—they all became more important when choosing a pillow from the Hug-Me Pillow Factory than the noble elf's wish to comfort a newborn baby for the rest of his or her life. Discomfort and greed were born. Elves no longer existed.

There are plenty of quotes by famous and less-famous people about self-respect. I would like to recall just some for this chapter:

- "Never esteem anything as of advantage to you that will make you break your word or lose your self-respect." (Marcus Aurelius)
- "Self-respect permeates every aspect of your life." (Joe Clark)
- "To free us from the expectations of others, to give us back to ourselves—there lies the great, singular power of self-respect." (Joan Didion)
- "If you want to be respected by others, the great thing is to respect yourself. Only by that, only by self-respect will you compel others to respect you." (Fyodor Dostoyevsky)
- "They cannot take away our self-respect if we do not give it to them." (Mahatma Gandhi)

- "Self-respect cannot be hunted. It cannot be purchased. It is never for sale. It cannot be fabricated out of public relations. It comes to us when we are alone, in quiet moments, in quiet places, when we suddenly realize that, knowing the good, we have done it; knowing the beautiful, we have served it; knowing the truth we have spoken it." (Whitney Griswold)
- "The world we have created is a product of our thinking; it cannot be changed without changing our thinking." (Albert Einstein)
- "A man can stand a lot as long as he can stand himself." (Axel Munthe)
- "If I despised myself, it would be no compensation if everyone saluted me, and if I respect myself, it does not trouble me if others hold me lightly." (Max Nordau)
- "Would that there were awards for people who come to understand the concept of enough: Good enough; successful enough; thin enough; rich enough; socially responsible enough. When you have self-respect, you have enough." (Gail Sheehy)

And last but not least:

- "Who we are looking for is who is looking." (St. Francis of Assissi)

Let's remember the first chapters of this book. I spoke of the "I-thou" relationship in this world between a mother and a child in conjunction with Martin Buber's theories. I wonder, at this point in the book, if a newborn still perceives a sense of respect for humankind from today's young mothers to grow into one person that then can give out respectful thoughts later on, as well. After all, love in itself, according to Buber, is already a subject relationship. In other words, have we become accustomed to being in love with love instead of with a newborn child? But if we don't share this love with somebody else, then we cannot share the unity of *being,* either.

I ask every mother who is reading this book to remember how her child or children came about. What were the primary reasons for wanting to become a mother? In a short questionnaire, I gave the following questions to about thirty mothers I came across:

1) Did you want to become a mother because you and your husband agreed that it would be lovely to strengthen your marital bond, and with that, to extend your family?
2) Did you want to become a mother because you liked the idea of nurturing a newborn and taking care of somebody?
3) Did you want to become a mother because you wanted something that belonged to you?
4) Did you want to become a mother of a girl or a boy?
5) Did you want to become a mother because you wanted to safe your marriage?
6) Did you want to become a mother because of the financial gain of receiving child's benefits?
7) Did you become a mother of two or more because you felt that your only child needed playmates?

The majority of answers related to questions 2 and 3; the rest were equally proportioned, except question 6, which was confirmed once. The need to care for somebody and the need for belonging was obvious. Out of the thirty mothers, about ten did not want to become mothers in the first place; it just happened. This questionnaire was not at all about wanting to put judgment onto mothers but was purely done for reasons of curiosity regarding self-respect and self-love.

If we truly are who we are, then we also encompass a belonging. But if we are or have become what was expected of us, then this innate sense of belonging seems to go astray. And with that, I truly believe we also lose self-respect. Too much has been brought along into this life to respect the reasons why we came into this life. From the moment we are born, we are looked at, or subjected to *respecere*. We are respected, and with that, we have gained self-respect. It is up to our growing-up process to strengthen this self-respect or to lose it altogether. In saying that, I don't personally believe we ever lose self-respect—this very unity of being—but it might go astray as too many demands are put our way. We are human beings, and we can only deal with so much.

Has the beginning of industrialization and pluralism in economic societies taken away this very unity of being and replaced it with a fake one, as in the Hug-Me Pillow fable? Though pluralism is the general sense—the acknowledgement—of diversity, it promotes the anonymous being with equal strength. In politics, pluralism is often considered by proponents of modern democracy to be in the interests of its citizens, and so political pluralism is one of its most important features. In the case of Norway, as described in the previous chapter, this most important feature has left one young man pretty lost in its own society. Although pluralism in democratic politics is a guiding principle which permits the peaceful co-existence of different interests, convictions, and lifestyles and considers it imperative that members of a society accommodate their differences by engaging in good-faith negotiations, it also failed in the September 11 events in New York ten years ago.

It seems paradoxical that one of the earliest arguments for pluralism came from America. James Madison was the fourth President of the United States between 1809 and 1817. He feared that factionalism would lead to fighting in the new American republic. Little did he know that his country a century later would become a target of this very thing. Pluralism hasn't done so well after all. Yes, pluralism is connected with the hope that a process of conflict and dialogue will lead to a definition and subsequent realization of the common good that is best for all members of society. But this implies also that in a pluralistic framework, the common good is not given a priority. Instead, the scope and content of the common good can only be found after the process of negotiation (i.e., a posterior.) Thinking of it, couldn't we apply the same for respect? Wouldn't respect be the common goal?

Still, one group may eventually manage to establish its own view as the generally accepted view, but only as the result of the negotiation process within the pluralistic framework. And this implies that as a general rule, the operator of a truly pluralistic framework (i.e., the state in a pluralistic society) must not be biased. It may not take sides with, give undue privileges to, or discriminate against any one group. Now, as all these operators as just an anonymous unit with human beings in their midst, how can such anonymous operators stay biased? Also, how can they stay respectful?

Of course, advocates of pluralism argue that this negotiation process is the best way to achieve the common goal, since everyone can participate in power and decision-making and claim part of the ownership of the results of exercising power. The focus is set on widespread participation and a greater feeling of commitment from society members—and therefore, a better outcome. This is all prevented in an authoritarian society where power is concentrated and decisions are made by just a few members. Arguments can be made for or against pluralism; the fact remains that in its authority, it stays anonymous. For pluralism to function at its best and be successful in defining the common goal, all groups have to agree to minimal consensus regarding shared values which tie the different groups to society and shared rules for conflict resolution between the groups. This sounds simple by merely reading it, but it remains a near-unachievable task, as by now our societies have grown bigger and closer together.

Even in pluralism, the most important value is that of mutual respect and tolerance so that different groups can coexist and interact without being forced to take on board anyone else's position in conflicts that will naturally arise out of diverging interests and positions. These conflicts can only be resolved durably by dialogue, the supporters of pluralism say. The dialogue hopefully leads to compromise and mutual understanding. History has shown that such compromises can be very lethal, and mutual understanding remains on paper (if at all).

In the ultimate consequence, pluralism (in my understanding) also would then imply the democratic right for individuals to determine values and truths for themselves instead of being forced to follow the whole of society, or indeed, their own group. And it is on that level of individuality that the arguments against pluralism arise. Because we have seen and experienced in all of the twentieth century that when individuals of a pluralistic economic society determine values and truths for themselves and resist being forced to follow the whole of society, then chaos develops, and horrible atrocities occur. We will not speak of those political times when one could not even resist being forced to follow the whole society out of fear becoming a deadly sufferer to the same.

August 2011 also saw the London riots. Many news-watchers, including New Zealanders, were caught up in the British riots, with some telling a New Zealand news channel of their disbelief as they watched the violence unfold in front of them. The news channel said that tens of thousands of Kiwis live in the UK, especially in the greater London area, which had seen some of the worst destruction. New Zealanders were advised to avoid areas where civil unrest was occurring and to follow any instructions issued by the local authorities. On TV NZ's website, New Zealanders were asked to report if they had witnessed the riots. And many Kiwis did respond to this call. One reported, "I can confirm a shop is on fire, and two hundred youths that gathered in the city have been chased by riot police and dispersed. Seven arrests have been made so far."

Far across the ocean, we learnt that a building near Salford was also set on fire by groups of youths. Rioters threw bricks at police and set fire to buildings in the city, and a BBC cameraman was assaulted. Television pictures showed flames leaping from shops and cars in both Salford and Manchester and plumes of thick black smoke billowing across roads.

Further south, in West Bromwich and Wolverhampton, cars were burned and stores raided. The looting violence caused one death after a man was shot. BBC said the twenty-six-year-old man was involved in a car chase and shot following an altercation with a group of about nine other men. Two men were arrested and bailed over the death. While London was waiting anxiously, not really knowing what was going on, the Metropolitan Police launched an investigation into the fatality. Up to sixteen thousand police officers were patrolling London's streets as a sense of fear and nervousness swept the city. Commuters hurried home early, shops shut, and many shopkeepers boarded their windows as the city prepared for a possible fourth night of violence that flared in neighbourhoods across London and other cities. In Hackney, the scene of some of the worst rioting, groups of yellow-vested police were visible everywhere. Gangs ransacked stores, carrying off clothes, shoes, and electronic goods; torched cars, shops, and homes, causing tens of millions of pounds of damage; and of course, taunted the police. Needless to say, a high degree of real fear and nervousness in and around London was felt, and anger and frustration were the result. This was not only directed at the youths involved in the riots but also at the police, despite the fact that already 563 arrests had been made by then and 105 people had been charged.

After all, people expect to be kept safe in their community, homes, and businesses. But even having ramped up their numbers significantly in London, the police still had to face high expectations. The level of violence clearly took the Met by surprise, and officers repeatedly described the scale of the riots as "unprecedented." Britain's Prime Minister announced, "This is criminality, pure and simple, and it has to be confronted and defeated." After a crisis meeting, he said, "People should be in no doubt that we will do everything necessary to restore orders to Britain's streets." *[49]

In Britain—as well as everywhere in the world, including here in New Zealand—people seemed to be at an utter loss as to where this violence came from. The trigger was when one man in Britain was shot by the police. The shooting appeared to have triggered a disastrous outcry of disrespect towards authorities. In the course of trying to understand what had happened, community leaders came to the conclusion that the violence in London—the worst for decades in the huge, multi-ethnic capital—was rooted in growing disparities in wealth and opportunities.

Through the days of the riots of London, I followed some people's opinions on the social networks. Comments such as those in the following list could be read:

1) Goodness, yes; I do believe it's time for our governments to take a step back and realize the people are sick of the stupid and selfish antics of politics and start appeasing the people who are really the backbone of the nation.

2) And you do that by setting fire to people's homes or shops? If they have something against the government, then attack the government buildings, not people at home!

3) It is beyond "teaching a lesson" now; people are joining in like sheep! It is hideous to watch, and you aren't earning respect at all. Pull your f—cking heads in and realize you look like absolute idiots.

4) I am from Tunisia, and I was there when everything started. *After* taking down the government, people started burning and breaking into shops and other people's property, but there was no police or army to stop them for three days. What we did—we organized ourselves, and we protected the streets; we kicked the ass of every son of a bitch that allowed himself to betray his country and set fire to a public or private property. I wished I lived in London. I will go down, and I will do my best to clean up the streets of this scam waste of time thugs.

5) No one is going to listen to you as you destroy people's homes and injure their families. Why not petition instead of this crap!!!!

6) Get the Swat Team.

7) Greetz from Ger! *Riot! Smash capitalism!* The city is yours.

8) Bring out the plastic bullets, water cannons; bloody attack them, no matter what the law says. 1's down; 1000s to come.

9) There's been a call to spread this shit into Liverpool. It's in Manchester, Salford, and spreading south now. They could shut down texting. Cut off the damn communications network that allows organization by anarchist scumbags that live off the government.

10) They are always demanding "respect." You don't demand respect; *you earn* it by thoughtful, considerate, peaceable actions. Ought to start lynching the sons of bitches.

11) I think they have tried that; didn't work. Now we are only following the examples our governments have set forth against other nations and the outrageous policies set forth on the people they are supposed to represent . . .

One lady from Scotland wrote to me, saying:

Eve, it's madness in the UK. So far, Scotland is trouble-free. I don't think there is one cause. England is very different [from] Scotland. Up here, we still have a little community spirit and society. For many years down south, things have been getting worse. We don't have a huge racial mix here. But in London, we see six-year-olds in school classes filled with twenty-five children, all speaking a different language. Most of them don't know the English language from the word "go." The police down south, we hear, had been involved in all sorts of corruption and bad treatments around youngsters. The few bad eggs, I may call them, make all of a sudden seem *all* [are] bad. Then there is unemployment. There are people not actually wanting to work. There are a lot of homeless people, and it has become a two-tier society, with very, very rich and very, very poor people. So, along comes criminality.

In short, Eve, there are too many things happening all at once, and people are just waiting for a reason to explode—that is, to riot. I don't want to make excuses for the rioters with this

observation. But this should never have happened. People have
lost their homes, are burnt out, lost their jobs, their business;
they have been beaten up at home and at work—for what? Just
for looting and money? It is a horror story, that's for sure. But
it is a very complex situation. Now, our wonderful governments
are going to set up yet another inquiry—yet another one to go
along with the few hundred already been in process. It will take
months or years to report and millions of £s wasted yet again.
And the bad thing will be that at the end of it, no one will know
what this was all about in the first place. When I was young, it
was called "brushing under the carpet."

Brushing under the carpet—is that the practice of a pluralistic economic
society in which nobody is able to respond any longer? In other words,
does no one exercise responsibility? The dialogues that came through the
social networks gave us the impression of helplessness and frustration. If
helplessness and frustration are felt with the adult world in the UK, how
much helplessness and frustration will be felt throughout the rows of the
younger generation?

I have touched on the pluralistic economic society quite a bit in the
process of this book. We have looked at the means and origins of pluralism.
I would like to take time now to look at the economic side of the matter.

Economy, in laymen's terms, is the social outcome of many people's
desires for material goods and services being met by their production
of these goods and services. The resulting goods and services then have
measurable value. Everybody knows that. An economy consists of the
economic system of a country or regional area; the labour, capital, and
land resources; and the economic agents that socially participate in the
production, exchange, distribution, and consumption of these goods and
services. Economy isn't just a thing; it is a process. This process involves
technological evolution, history, and social organization as well as its
geography, natural resource endowment, and ecology as main factors.

And it is those factors that ultimately give context and content and set the conditions and parameters in which an economy functions. We mentioned economic agents before. These include all professions and occupations, from social science to sociology; from history and anthropology to geography; from production, distribution, and exchange to consumption; from engineering to management and business administration; and all other not-mentioned economic activities contributing to the economy. Consumption, saving, and investment are core variable components in any given economy and determine the market equilibrium—the balance or stability of the economy. Economic activities are further divided into three categories: primary, secondary, and tertiary activities.

I could trace the English terms "economy" and "economics" back to the Greek words (1) "one who manages a household," "*οἰκονόμος*," derived from "house" *(οἶκος)* and "distribute" *(νέμω)* in the meaning of managing, (2) "household management," "*οἰκονομία*," and (3) "of a household or family," "*οἰκονομικός*."

Interestingly enough, the first recorded sense of the word "economy" was "the management of economic affairs" within a monastery, possibly composed in a work around 1440. Years later, the term "economy" was recorded in more general senses, such as "thrift" and "administration." But the most frequently used current sense, "the economic system of a country or a local area," seems to have developed only recently during the nineteenth and twentieth centuries.

From my school years of economics, I learnt that as long as someone has been making, supplying, and distributing goods or services, there has been some sort of economy. Over time, economies grew larger and larger as societies grew and hence became more complex. Between 4500-4000 BC, the Sumer had developed a large-scale economy based on commodity money while the Babylonians and their neighbouring city states later between 1750-1595 BC developed the earliest system of economics as we think of it today in terms of rules and laws on debt, legal contracts, and law codes relating to business practices and private property. The Babylonians, along with their city state neighbours, started to develop forms of economics comparable to currently used social concepts. They also created the first known codified legal and administrative systems, complete with courts, jails, and government records.

Several centuries after the invention of the ancient writing system of cuneiform, the use of writing expanded beyond debt and payment certificates. Inventory lists were applied for the first time, about 2600BC, to messages and mail deliveries, history, legends, mathematics, astronomical records, and other pursuits.

For the first time in history, ways to divide private property were standardized, as was any form of compensation in money for different infractions of formalized law. The ancient economy was primarily based on subsistence farming. The shekel, a coin of eleven grams or thirty-five troy ounces, referred to a unit of weight and currency with its first appearance in the Mesopotamia around 3000 BC. It referred to a specific mass of barley, which again related other values in metric, such as silver, bronze, copper, etc. Originally a barley/shekel was both a unit of currency and a unit of weight; just as later the British pound was originally a unit denominating a one-pound mass of silver.

The exchange of goods started for most people through their social relationships. But there were also traders who bartered in the marketplaces. In ancient Greece, many people were bond slaves of the freeholders. Let's remember that the present term "economy" originated in Greece. Economic discussion was driven by scarcity—the fundamental economic problem of having seemingly unlimited human needs and wants in a world of limited resources. Scarcity indicates that a society has insufficient productive resources to fulfil all human wants and needs. On the other hand, it was also well-known that not all of society's goals could be pursued at the same time, and trade-offs would be made of one good against others.

Between 384-322 BC, Aristotle was the first to differentiate between a use value and an exchange value of goods. The exchange ratio he defined was not only the expression of the value of goods but of the relations between the people involved in trade. For most of the time in history, economy, therefore, stood always in opposition to institutions with fixed exchange ratio as reign, state, religion, culture, and tradition.

What we now call economy was actually not very far from the subsistence level in medieval times. Most exchange occurred within social groups, but on top of this, the great conquerors raised the so-called venture capital to finance their captures. This capital would be refunded by the goods they would bring up in the New World.

And much later, the first banks were founded. The discoveries of Marco Polo, Christopher Columbus, and Vasco da Gama led to a first global economy. In response to this global growth, Giovanni di Bicci de Medici founded his bank during 1360-1428 and Jakob Fugger his during 1459-1525. Already in 1513, the first stock exchange was founded in Antwerp, the Netherlands. Economy at those times changed its meaning to trade, primarily. The European captures became branches of the European states, which they called colonies, and trade grew even more diverse in its economic use. Spain, Portugal, France, Great Britain, and the Netherlands—all rising nations under the establishment of colonies—then tried to control their trade through custom duties and taxes. They felt through these, they could protect their national economy. The first approach to intermediate between private wealth and public interest came into existence and was called mercantilism.

At this point, we have to refer back to religious values, as a transformation happened known under the term "secularization." I believe this to have been a very important part of a society's identification and self-worth. Secularization is the transformation of a society from close identification with religious values and institutions toward non-religious, or irreligious, values and secular institutions. A new belief was born.

A society progresses particularly through modernization and rationalism, and religion loses its authority in all aspects of social life and governance. Social theorists have long postulated that the modernization of a society would include a decline in levels of religiosity. But some theorists also argue that the secularization of modern civilization partly would result from our human inability to adapt broad ethical and spiritual needs of mankind to the increasingly fast advance of the physical sciences. Be the argument as it is, the fact was that through the secularization in Europe, states were allowed to use the immense property of the church for the development of towns. It is no surprise to learn that the influence of the so-called nobles consequently decreased.

Later in the seventeenth and eighteenth centuries, the first Secretaries of State for economy started their work, and bankers like Rothschild started to finance national projects, such as wars and infrastructure. And again, the meaning of the word "economy" changed. From then on, "economy" meant a national economy as a topic for the economic activities of the citizens of a state.

The first economist in the true meaning of the word was the Scotsman Adam Smith (1723-1790). He defined the elements of a national economy as products that are offered at a natural price generated by the use of competition, supply and demand, and the division of labour. He maintained throughout his life that the basic for free trade has to be human self-interest. Consequently, the so-called self-interest hypothesis became the anthropological basis for economics. At about the same time, the Reverend Thomas Malthus, an English scholar who was influential in political economy and demography of his time, not only popularized the economic theory of rent, but also transferred the idea of supply and demand to the problem of overpopulation during the times of the Industrial Revolution. The United States of America became the place where millions of expatriates from all European countries began searching for free economic evolvement. This is a paradox to what we know of America today, isn't it? After all, until only recently, before the global recession, the US economy was known to be the largest national economy, with an estimated 2010 GDP of $13,780 trillion—23 percent of the nominal global GDP and 20 percent of the global GDP at purchasing power parity.

The Industrial Revolution was a period from the eighteenth to nineteenth centuries when major changes in agriculture, manufacturing, mining, and transport had a profound effect on the socioeconomic and cultural conditions. It started in the UK, and from there, it spread throughout Europe, North America, and eventually, the world.

The onset of this Industrial Revolution marked a major turning point in human history; almost every aspect of daily life was eventually influenced in some way. In Europe, the system of mercantilism was replaced by wild capitalism, and this led to economic growth. The term "industrial revolution" was created, as the system of production and division of labour enabled the mass production of goods.

Then WWI and WWII came and ended. With resultant chaotic times and a devastating Great Depression, policymakers searched for new ways of controlling the course of economy. Friedrich von Hayek and Milton Friedman pleaded for a global Free Trade and can be looked at as the fathers of the so-called neoliberalism. Hayek was an Austrian-Hungarian economist and philosopher and became known for his defence of classical liberalism and free market capitalism against the socialist and collectivist thoughts of the time. In 1974, he won the Nobel Memorial Prize in Economic Sciences. Hayek served in WWI and believed that his experience in the war and desire to help avoid the mistakes that led to the war led him consequently to his career. The Great Depression became the marking point of his career. Hayek lived in Austria, Great Britain, the United States, and Germany. Most of his academic life was spent at the London School of Economics, the University of Chicago, and the University of Freiburg.

Friedman was an American economist, statistician, academic, and author who taught at the University of Chicago for more than three decades. He also was a recipient of a Nobel Memorial Prize in Economic Sciences. He was best known for his theoretical and empirical research— especially consumption analysis, monetary history, and theory—and for his demonstration of the complexity of stabilization policy. He became the economic advisor to US President Ronald Reagan. Over time, many governments practiced his restatement of a political philosophy that extolled the virtues of a free market economic system with little intervention by government. Friedman became the most influential economist of the second half of the twentieth century, and some argue, possibly of the entire century.

However, there was also John Maynard Keynes, a British economist, whose ideas have profoundly affected the theory and practice of modern macroeconomics as well as the economic policies of governments. Keynes worked on the causes of business cycles and advocated the use of fiscal and monetary measures to mitigate the adverse effects of economic recessions and depressions. His Keynesian economics became world-renowned. Already in the 1930s, Keynes spearheaded a revolution in economic thinking, overturning the older ideas of neoclassical economics that held that free markets would, in the short to medium term, automatically provide full employment as long as workers were flexible in their wage demands. Instead, Keynes argued that aggregate demand determined the overall level of economic activity and that inadequate aggregate demand could lead to prolonged periods of high unemployment. Following the outbreak of WWII, Keynes's ideas concerning economic policy were adopted by leading Western economies. During the 1950s and 1960s, the success of the Keynesian economics resulted in almost all capitalist governments adopting his policy recommendations, promoting the cause of social liberalism.

In the 1970s, Keynes's influence waned. Let's not forget that the 70s can be recalled as a time of rebirthing—a renaissance for people's needs to go back to nature. The hippie culture seems to have grown out of nowhere, and the first negative tumults against capitalism became visible. With the Industrial Revolution and the later need for economic leaders and politicians to regulate and control the stability of their economy, individuality in the societies had long faded away, and the labourers and workers became anonymous. Mass production had its identity in the mass, and a culture and country lost its identity as well. But without identity, is any form of respect liveable? The new god to pray to was the economy—in short, money. In addition, multiculturalism set in. Foreign workers were imported into European countries that had lost their hard-working men during WWII and desired a better lifestyle. The young generation post-WWII became academically orientated, and the need for labourers pushed foreign boundaries. The pluralistic society became a socioeconomic one.

From the start of the 1970s, problems began to afflict the Anglo-American economies, partly because of critiques from Friedman and other economists who were pessimistic about the ability of governments to regulate the business cycle with fiscal policy. However, the arrival of the global financial crisis in 2007 caused a resurrection in Keynesian thought.

The call for identity in the 70s died out pretty quickly. A pluralistic economic society did not allow individuality to emerge. Thirty years later, Keynesian economics provided a theoretical underpinning for economic policies undertaken in response to the crisis by the US Presidents George W. Bush and Barack Obama and by Prime Minister Gordon Brown of the UK, as well as by other global leaders. The Wikipedia on Answers.com informs in length about Keynes and his economic career and mentions that in 1999, *Time* magazine wrote the following", "Keynes's radical idea that governments should spend money they don't have may have saved capitalism" and included him in their list of the 100 most important and influential people of the twentieth century. [*50]

Keynes was always a very complex person, and in addition to being an economist, he also was a civil servant, the director of the Bank of England, a patron of the arts, and an art collector. Additionally, he was known as an advisor to several charitable trusts, a writer, a private investor, and a farmer. In 1925, he married the Russian ballerina Lydia Lopokova but never had children of his own. In most countries, an economic system is called a social market economy, and in nearly all of them, pluralism plays a central role.

In the beginning, I mentioned that we can divide economy into three stages—the primary, secondary, and tertiary stage—but we can now even add a fourth—a quaternary stage.

In the primary stage, we look at the process of extraction and production of raw materials, such as corn, coal, wood, and iron. The coal miner or the fisherman as workers in this primary stage are referred to as personnel resources in today's economies.

The secondary stage of the economy involves the transformation of raw or intermediate materials into goods, such as manufacturing steel into cars or textiles into clothing. The builder or a dressmaker would be personnel resources in this second stage, in which the associated industrial economy is additionally sub-divided into several economic industries. These subdivisions evolved during the Industrial Revolution.

The tertiary stage involves mainly the provision of services to consumers and business, such as baby-sitting, cinemas, or banking. Shopkeepers and accountants would be the personnel resources in this stage.

The fourth stage occupies research and development needed to produce products from natural resources with their following into products. A logging company might research ways to use partially burnt wood, as an example, to be processed so that the undamaged portions of it can be made into pulp for paper. Education can be part of this quaternary stage.

Other sectors of the developed community include the public or state sector, such as parliament, law courts, government centres, emergency services, public health, transport facilities, hospitals, libraries, museums, recreational parks and gardens or reserves, sports stadiums, concert halls and theatres, and centres for various religions. Then we have the private sector, with privately run businesses, and a social sector or voluntary sector.

All these economic activities need a way to be measured. Without going into too much detail about these measuring methods, the most important methods to mention are consumer spending, the exchange rate, the GDP (gross domestic product), the GDP per capita, the stock market, interest rates, national debt, inflation rate, unemployment, and the balance of trade. The GDP includes only economic activities for which money is exchanged. In other words, the GDP is a measure of the size of a nation's economy.

The subdivision in the secondary stage into several economic industries plays a vital part of the whole of economies. In today's understanding, we mostly identify an industry by its product, such as the chemical industry, petroleum industry, automotive industry, electronic industry, meatpacking industry, hospitality industry, food and fish industries, software industry, paper industry, semiconductor industry, entertainment industry, cultural industry, poverty industry, and many more.

The Industrial Revolution led to the development of factories for mass production. Consequently, there were changes in society. Originally, factories were steam-powered, but they later transitioned to electricity once an electrical grid was developed. The mechanized assembly line was introduced to assemble parts in repeatable fashion, with workers each performing specific steps during this process. This led to significant increases in efficiency, lowering the cost of the end process. That meant that personnel resources were easily burnt out for the common good of the economy. Not much later, automation was increasingly used to replace personnel resources—again for the common good of the economy. Not only individuality, but also the value of each person faded out, once having been in the process for the common good of their society. The common good became the economy (e.g., the GPD it could produce). The process then accelerated with the development of the computer and the robot.

It becomes obvious that historically, certain manufacturing industries have by now gone into decline due to various economic factors, including the development of replacement technology or the loss of competitive advantage. A simple example is the decline in manufacturing carriages made place to the automobile industry with its mass production. A very recent trend became transparent through the migration of prosperous, industrialized nations towards a post-industrial society. This happened as a nation passed through a phase of society predominated by a manufacturing-based economy and moved on to a structure of a society based on the provision of information, innovation, finance, and services. The so-called information revolution was born, and manufacturing was relocated to economically more favourable locations through a process called off-shoring.

Traditionally, success was measured in the number of jobs created. With the development of replacement technologies, one assumed this to cause the decline in the competitiveness of the sector. The truth, however, was that it was caused by the introduction of the so-called lean manufacturing process. Lean, essentially, is centred on preserving value with less work. Lean manufacturing has been a management philosophy mostly derived from the Toyota Production System. Some, therefore, refer to this as Toyotism; it was only identified as lean in the 1990s. So it's still a very young manufacturing process (if you can call it manufacturing in the essence of the word). Toyota initially focused on reduction of the original Toyota seven wastes to improve overall customer value, but there still are varying perspectives on how this is best achieved. Toyota has steadily grown from a small company to the world's largest automaker and has focused attention on how it achieved this. Again, it becomes transparent that the individual value of a worker has completely faded into the background, and success is not measured any longer in the number of jobs that can be created but in the improvement of overall customer value.

Eventually, this shift towards overall customer value could lead to competing product lines being managed by one of two people, as is already the case in the cigarette manufacturing industry. Related to this change is the upgrading of the quality of the manufactured produce. While it is easy to produce a low-tech, low-skill product, the ability to manufacture high-quality products remains limited to companies with a highly-skilled staff. It has been an overall realization not only within the manufacturing industries but also within the line of customers, which again consists of individuals, that after the miracle economic years of post-WWII ended, reality set in. The quality of products started to lack in all areas, including the service area, which had become a specialized industry after the decline of the post-WWII miracle economic years. Mercedes, for instance, still produced a quality car that now had to guarantee a constant demand for maintenance and servicing. This was supposed to guarantee a long-term profit for the company. The focus on service became a very important avenue for profit, but quality service, needless to say, also required quality, skilled staff.

During the 1980s and even more so during the 1990s, European countries were faced with the fact that not only quality workers had faded from their industries, but also excellent academics who left their home industries and went into countries with better pay. In order to strengthen Europe's fiscal situation, the Euro was created. The Euro failed to keep its promise for a better financial bond within Europe. To the contrary, Europe is by now suffering from the worst recession ever. But so is America, in its own right, due to overspending.

An ever-alluring, sanctimonious buffet presented by industries worldwide in a greedy, consumer-driven word finally revealed itself to the consumers as an illusion towards the promise of making one feel good. It had done exactly the opposite. It had made people unhappy, frustrated, and helpless—and yes, a lot of us are also aggressive and have utter disrespect for whoever tells us what we should or should not do.

The moment we come into this life—already in the first steps of being an embryo in our mothers' wombs—we start learning, as our senses become more and more tuned to do what they are meant to do—sensing through skin contact, seeing through the eyes, listening through the ears, tasting through our tongues, and then ultimately responding from a balanced gut feeling. But the moment we become part of our societies' sanctimonious buffets, we are mislead by their constant presence, no matter whether we ask for it or not. The balance of demand and need, in my opinion, is completely out of sync and needs readdressing. I feel this could be done by a mere look at self-respect. It could challenge everybody who lives in this avenue of illusion.

I have purposely taken some time to explore the meanings of pluralism and economy and the paths they have taken from their existence. I hope I can make the illusion of all of it more transparent. As long as we *respicere*—that is, look back at—how we can achieve only one side of the beauty-and-beast package which promises us good feelings and ignores that feeling bad is part of a whole being, we will continue living in this avenue of illusion. We need to accept the whole package—look at it for what it is and then respect it. And that includes us as human beings all the same.

In a very paradoxical way, this very pious buffet has made the bad side of humanity very transparent. The human being has become overwhelmed, helpless, and frustrated. We might judge this as bad, but in the end, isn't still having the ability to become overwhelmed, helpless, and frustrated the simple yet intrepid nature of being human? The response of the individuality in form of the valued customer within a pluralistic economic society is finally daring to make itself visible. Even if it mostly appears to do that in the shape of what we call the youth, it still has a voice and an appearance.

Nobody is perfect. As long as moral teachers and various forms of religions are demanding of us to live perfectly, we shall fail. We are not perfect—or, better said, we are as perfect as the ambivalence of good and bad as a whole.

When I was trained as a psychotherapist, we were given a story of a father who mourned his son, who appeared to have become a soul without any respect despite his teachings. The father wrote a long letter to a friend, and this letter was read to us. We had to guess who this father could have been and to which century he might have belonged. It was obvious that we were in the middle of discussing the ever-existing and ever-returning myth of generational conflict or the generation gap. Nobody in our discussion panel came to the right conclusion. No, the letter was not written by an industrial of the Industrial Revolution or a Mr. Rothschild of modern times. It was, in fact, written by Aristotle, the great Greek philosopher, student of Plato, and teacher of Alexander the Great.

Aristotle lived from 384-322 BC. That is how long the generation conflict has existed, though the term "generation gap" was popularized in Western countries during the 1960s. It was then that people increasingly and openly referred to differences between people of a younger generation and their elders, especially between a child and his or her parent's generation. Let's be reminded that the 1960s were the high times of the post-WWII miracle economic years. Of course, some generational differences had existed throughout history; but with more rapid cultural and economic change during the modern era, differences between the two generations increased in comparison to previous times, particularly with respect to such matters as musical tastes, fashion, culture, and politics. It might have also been magnified by the then-unprecedented size of the young generation during the 1960s, which gave it unparalleled power and willingness to rebel against societal norms. Bob Dylan's song "The Times They Are a Changin'" and the 1965 hit "My Generation" by The Who reflected very well such conflicts between the generations.

As the 1940s ended and the 1950s emerged, a marked difference between teenagers and parents also emerged. The dating system transformed. The new medium of television gained widespread popularity and often portrayed teenagers as juvenile delinquents before the war in Southeast Asia changed towards another appearance in young people. Remember, JDs followed the standard black. JD, short for J.D. Salinger was the hero in Holden Caulfield's 1951 novel *The Cather in the Rye* and became a literary embodiment of teenage angst and alienation further fueling adults' perception of teenagers as rebels. The saying became "black is beautiful" and coincided with a cultural movement that began in the United States of America in the 1960s by African Americans.

The trend of going steady and marrying early became the norm in the 40s, compared to the times before the war, when a "rating and dating" trend was a lot more fashionable. The mid—and late 1960s gave rise to the hippie culture, with diverging opinions about the draft and military involvement in Vietnam along with an elevated use of drugs. Drugs became a significant topic of the generation gap of this area. "Make love, not war" and "MAD widens the generation gap" were printed everywhere. Men started to wear long hair to refer to a role model of Jesus.

In and after 1964, something changed. The widespread influence of the Beatles and their 1964 film *A Hard Day's Night* contributed to the generation gap in that the Beatles became role models who observed and articulated the shortcomings of adults.

The world-renowned TV series *All In the Family* was originally broadcast on CBS from January 1971 to April 1978. The show ranked number one in the yearly Nielsen ratings from 1971-1976 and became the first television series to reach the milestone of having toppled the Nielsen rating for five consecutive years, a mark previously unmatched. Archie Bunker, the show's protagonist, was named TV's greatest character of all time. A new show picked up where *All In the Family* ended. The new show's title was *Archie Bunker's Place,* and it lasted another four years until 1983. It was definitely

Archie Bunker—this very conservative-minded, middle-aged man—and his repeated quarrels with his independent-minded wife, a staunchly liberal daughter, and a son-in-law which made this show the success it was. The show as produced by Norman Lear and was based on the British television comedy series *Till Death Do Us Part*. In its depiction of issues previously considered unsuitable for the US network television comedy, such as racism, homosexuality, women's liberation, rape, miscarriage, abortion, breast cancer, the Vietnam War, menopause, and impotence, *All In the Family* dealt with everything the viewers had to deal with in the 70s. And Alfred Bunker addressed it. Another role model was born.

In the 1980s, a generation out of the 1970s grew stronger, and they were called Generation X. The 1970s and 1980s became known as an area rampant with child neglect, as shown by such phenomenon as the so-called latchkey kids. Latchkey kids are those who had to return from school to an empty home because their parents were away at work. Children often were left home with little or no parental supervision. The pious buffet I mentioned before made this side of human neglect also very transparent. A house key was often strung around the child's neck or left hidden under a mat at the rear door to the property. During the times of magic worldwide economic recovery, frustration of the same started to become visible. People still refused to look back—*respicere*—to 1944, when children were forced to stay home alone during and after WWII when one parent would be enlisted into the armed forces and the other would have to get a job. When the nation calls or the economy demands profit, it seems child neglect is a phenomenon that goes along with it. But the effects of being a latchkey child are still visible, though they may differ with age. Loneliness, boredom, and fear are common for those younger than ten years of age. During the early teens, there is obviously a greater susceptibility to peer pressure, potentially resulting in such behaviour as alcohol abuse, drug abuse, sexual promiscuity, and smoking.

If and when the loving eyes of mothers leave the child, no matter what age this child has reached, a sense of rejection in the child will be experienced, and all lessons of unconditional love will fade into the background. The world is bigger than Mum, and peer pressure gets its hold on the youngster. It is very well known today that socioeconomic status and length of time left alone can bring forth other negative effects. In one study, middle school students left home alone for more than three hours a day reported higher levels of behavioural problems, higher rates of depression, and lower levels of self-esteem than other students. "[51] If a child is not able to look at—*respecere*—his or her belonging within a family dynamic, it is no wonder that a loss of respect will also occur. Self-esteem and self-respect are not too far apart from their meanings. After all, self-esteem reflects a person's overall evaluation or appraisal of his or her own worth. Of course, it would encompass beliefs and emotions, such as "I am competent" and "I am worthy" versus "I am worthless: not even Mum or Dad care" or emerging emotions such as triumph, despair, pride, or shame.

Self-esteem, self-worth, self-regard, and self-integrity are all synonyms of self-respect. The *American Heritage Dictionary* of the English language says that self-love is "the instinct or desire to promote one's well-being." La Rochefoucauld, a noted French author of maxims and memoirs in the middle of the seventeenth century, considered that self-regard would be the mainspring of all human activities.

Children from lower-income families have commonly been associated with greater externalizing problems, such as conduct disorders, academic problems, and the ever-growing numbers in hyperactivity. The latter is even rising in higher-income families, while children from middle—and upper-class families supposedly are no different than their supervised peers. A 2000 German PISA (Programme for International Student Assessment) study, however, found no significant differences in the scholastic performance between latchkey kids and kids in a nuclear family, the latter referring to a family group consisting of a father, mother, and children all exclusively sharing living quarters. However, we don't want to give the positive outcome of our latchkey children a complete miss. Reportedly, a latchkey child feels independence and self-reliance at a young age. To me, though, independence and self-reliance are not markers towards gaining and keeping the value of self-respect.

Generation X was followed towards the late 80s to the present and is widely referred to as the baby-on-board, parenting-focused era. The 1980s along with the 1990s also produced the Null-Bock Generation, as children and teenagers alike were had no ambition to define what they actually wanted from life. The Null-Bock Generation very much stood for a lack of interest in anything that society generated and had to offer in one way or another.

Coincidentally or not, the post-WWII times also gave birth to the first terrorist groups. The Red Army Faction, better known as RAF, in its early stages was founded in 1970 by Andreas Baader, Gudrun Ensslin, Horst Mahler, and Ulrike Meinhof—commonly known as the Baader-Meinhof Group—was one of post-WWII Germany's most violent and prominent left-wing terror groups. The RAF described itself as a communist and anti-imperialist urban guerrilla group engaged in armed resistance against what they deemed to be a fascist state. The RAF committed numerous disastrous operations, which led to a national crisis in Germany. Its actions were responsible for thirty-four deaths, including many secondary targets, such as chauffeurs and bodyguards, and many injuries in its almost thirty years of activity.

During the 1990s and 2000s, many cultural differences concerning what should be a gender or sexual norm as well as new technology, political differences and indifferences, workplace behaviour, age of consent, age of responsibility, the education system in general, and many other political, cultural, and generational issues started to create generational frictions between Generation X and Generation Y along with their Baby Boomer parents. Generation Y became the label for the Millennial Generation. This started with the adolescents of the late 1980s. To me, it is no wonder that youth today are irritated and agitated. Over the last centuries, we all have become victims to pluralistic socioeconomic societies. By hoping to be able to do the only best for our children, we have, in fact, done the straight opposite.

Though it happened many years ago, I still can hear Thomas Huxley saying, "Do what you should do, when you should do it, whether you feel like it or not." These were biblical words towards success, but they also included a very important feature of human ability, and that was the feature of discipline. And discipline was the highest order of success. Huxley went on to say, "There are 999 other success principles that I have found in my reading and experience, but without self-discipline, none of them work." Huxley, the English biologist, was known as Darwin's Bulldog for his advocacy of Charles Darwin's theory of evolution.

Of course, such teachings of discipline for the purpose of economic success only did not have many listeners during the 1970s, when hippies and the like started to revolt against any kind of authority. Most did not even want to be reminded of the virtues of discipline. They been too much a part of many lives which had been connected to the traumas of WWI and WWII. No, if there was one thing that people yearned for, it was freedom and peace. The future, with all its consuming power, did promise just that. Cigarette and alcohol advertisements and all products within the leisure industry used the miracle words "freedom" and "peace" wherever they could.

Discipline, for a lot of our young people, was and still is, however, a language of the past. In today's books of conduct, discipline is of military and religious orders, where obeying is the first rule. But the same first rule could be applied in child discipline and self-discipline today for a better tomorrow in general, which I will explain more in detail later on. In its original sense, discipline mostly refers to systematic instruction given to disciples to train them as students in a craft or trade or to follow a particular code of conduct or order. It is very much a virtue that has lost its value and methods of use nearly completely over time other than in a clerical or military sense. Today, the phrase "to discipline" has a negative connotation to its social weight. Too often, the term "discipline" is connected to and regulated through punishment. However, to discipline does not mean anything more than to instruct somebody to follow a particular code of conduct or order, which is essential in avoiding chaos or anarchic tendencies. With a child, discipline means no more than referring to methods of modelling character and teaching self-control alongside acceptable behaviour. It should be as easy as teaching your child to wash her or his hands before meals, which will eventually develop into a pattern of behaviour. In other words, you have then disciplined your child to adapt to that pattern. This process of adapting is called growing up under the influence of training in self-discipline and self-help through every activity.

Richard Kemp, the president of the Bankers Management Incorporation, has thirty years of management experience in consulting, training credit administration, and new business development. He once said, "Without discipline, there is nothing to be proud of." [52] Unfortunately, over time, the need to maintain order has made the term "to discipline" more and more negative, as it carries the "must do" of ensuring instructions are indeed carried out. To be disciplined can subsequently be—subject to context, of course—either a virtue (an ability to follow instructions well) or a euphemism for punishment, which unfortunately mostly refers to disciplinary procedure. That merely strengthens the belief in and the connotation of negativity of the term "discipline."

Church discipline is a response of an ecclesiastical body to some perceived wrong, whether in action or in doctrine. Its most extreme form in modern churches is excommunication. Discipline here is the assertion of willpower over more base desires and is usually understood to be synonymous with self-control. Self-discipline can, to some extent, be seen as a substitute for motivation when one uses reason to determine a best course of action that opposes one's desires. Such virtuous behaviour is when one's motivations are aligned with one's reasoned aims—to do what one knows is best and to do it gladly. Continent behaviour, on the other hand, is when one does what one knows is best but must do it by opposing one's motivation. It is obvious that moving from continent to virtuous behaviour requires training and some self-discipline.

Self-discipline can, in my understanding, also be defined as the ability to motivate oneself in spite of a negative emotional state. Qualities associated with self-discipline hence include willpower, hard work, and persistence. How much of the latter has faded away within the societies of the last one hundred years through industrialization, computerization, and simply through an overwhelming set of principles of pluralistic socioeconomic societies? Where is self-respect in all that? We all need to look back at where we originally came from.

We are a part of the world's existence. And on the level of existence, we all deserve respect. As human beings, we have to start with self-respect and then go beyond and decide what else is out there that deserves respect. I think if we look closely enough, we shall find heaps to respect. We just need to start looking again beyond the segments of appearances, conditioned perceptions, and generally approved judgements.

Respect lies within. And within, we have to start looking.

> Human beings, by changing the inner attitudes of their minds, can change the outer aspects of their lives.
>
> **William James (1842-1910)**

WHO DESERVES IT?

The question, "Who deserves respect?" is not that easy to answer any longer, so it seems.

In our pluralistic, economic societies, it seems we fail to show respect to anybody. Nobody seems to live up to an idol, hero, or icon, and if the desire were present, it would be doomed from the word "go," as anything to aspire to seems to be connected with having the money to do so. Then again, we also see some very dim-witted behaviour that costs our communities money which could be used for much better causes.

In late August of 2011, for instance, an emergency police callout cost at least $10,000 (NZ) but ended up being a hoax. Police received a call at around 11:30 p.m. saying two young children were being assaulted by their parents in Clutha, about eighty kilometres southwest of Dunedin. The acting sergeant told NZPA the caller, a woman, said alcohol, drugs, and unsecured firearms had been involved in the incident. So this seemed to be a serious call which needed to be followed up. Twenty staff members were used to investigate. Five costly hours later, the investigation had to put it all down to a hoax, and a thirty-four-year-old Wanaka woman was charged.

In early August of 2011, a twenty-three-year-old student who had used an air rifle to send partygoers running and screaming received a severe telling off by the judge when he appeared for sentence. The young man had pled guilty to two firearms charges resulting from his stupid actions at a party in a suburb of Tauranga in the Bay of Plenty on 26 March, 2011. Needless to say, the student had been drinking and was asked to leave the party. Later he returned with an air rifle. He was arrested at the time, and when sober, he pleaded guilty to unlawfully carrying a firearm and unlawfully presenting a firearm. During sentencing, the judge reminded the offender of the recent Norwegian massacre, where a man killed seventy-six people with a gun. "I know you are not going to do that, but people at the party with you—they don't know what you are going to do. It is hugely frightening. That's why one of these charges carries a sentence of four years jail. If you didn't have personal health issues, I would have been considering jail or home detention; that's how serious this is."

After drinking at the party and being asked to leave, police say the young offender returned at about 1:30 a.m. with the air rifle with telescopic sights. He pointed the air rifle at partygoers, who screamed and ran, and then he waved the weapon in the air. A person at the party escorted the young man home, where armed police seized the air rifle soon afterwards. Through his lawyer, the offender said he didn't recall pointing the rifle at anyone. "It appears you were angry about what happened at a party—you were drunk," said the judge. "You went home still angry and returned with a firearm—an air rifle." He sentenced the student to supervision for twelve months with special conditions and ordered he perform three hundred hours of community work. The offender's fines were cancelled, and there is an order for the destruction of the air rifle.

Alcohol and drugs are known to lead to destructive behaviour. When rejections are perceived by an intoxicated person, related response actions can be rather lethal. But in both above examples, is alcohol or drug use to be blamed in the first place? I don't think so. It is the overall attitude that is to be blamed and certainly a complete lack of respect.

On 6 August, the news told New Zealanders that an elderly couple was found dead in their Nelson home two days after their death. The couple—aged eighty-four and eighty-eight—died in an apparent suicide. Police had been alerted by a visitor to the house that the couple hadn't been answering their door, and meals left at the address had not been taken inside. A Nelson police detective explained that police entered the house and found the elderly couple in an apparent assisted suicide. The investigation revealed that the couple had been members of the Nelson chapter of Exit International, a voluntary euthanasia group formed by Australian doctor Philip Nitschke. The euthanasia group's spokesman informed the Nelson Mail that the couple had indeed attended meetings of the group in the city. Through this involvement, they had acquired the knowledge they needed and also had indicated in one of their last group attendances that they wouldn't be joining any more for family reasons. The couple was perceived as very lovely, sweet, and gentle. They seemed devoted to each other and just felt that the life of one without the other wouldn't be worth it.

Yes, the topic of the elderly could fill a whole chapter on its own when it comes to respect. Recently I came across an article from 2008 in *The Fresno Bee* from California with the headline, "Senior-care industry expands with elderly population." A photo showing an elderly couple enjoying their exercise by hitting a beach ball at their assisted living home reflects fun and life-long joy. The article said that California's elderly population is expected to grow twice as fast as the rest of the state by 2020. And those in the senior care industry would be ready and waiting. Yes, I bet they are.

Competition in this multibillion-dollar market is brisk as existing providers jockey for customers and new companies open to join the fray. The coordinator of the Fresno/Madera Ombudsman Program said it boldly: "There is money to be made out there, and people know it." The industry publication *Private Duty Insider* estimated that the nine largest companies providing in-home care to seniors accounts for $1.4 billion in sales nationally in 2006 alone. Consequently, all sorts of entrepreneurs have been jumping into the market, as it promises to become huge with a growing older population. Nationally, the population over age sixty-five is expected to double within the next twenty-five years in the United States. By 2030, almost one in five Americans—an estimated 72 million people— will have reached the age of sixty-five and older. In Fresno County, the number of people over sixty is expected to increase 149 percent from 1990 to 2020. Already, those over the age of sixty represent 13.5 percent of the 1.1 million people in Fresno and Madera counties. [*53] Nursing homes are not the only options any longer for the elderly. Private companies that provide in-home care can help seniors stay in their homes. Seniors also can choose to move into country-club-like facilities. The options are endless.

Sorting out what's good for Mum or Dad is not simple to do. Compared to only half a century ago, we have to look at completely different situations of elderly disease, time budgeting, and family dynamics. Even some American workplaces now realize the need and provide elder care services to their employees. Many of the demands for professional elder care come from adults literally squeezed by their responsibility and remaining respect for both the parents and children. They care for both their own children and their elderly relatives. With advanced health and pharmaceutical industries focusing on the elderly, we are today faced with senior diseases we didn't even know they existed fifty years ago. Alzheimer's was hardly spoken of, and senility did not have the widespread spectrum of diagnosis it has today. Many adult children have been thrown into a carer role and are reaching out for help. They have lives, children of their own, and work. Our societies have all come to the conclusion that caring without having to spend money is not possible any longer. Those who have to make some tough decisions regarding the care of their parents are not in an easy situation, though many options are available. Some of the most popular options for family members to choose from are in-home care providers or residential care facilities.

Home Instead Senior Care is one of the leaders in the industry. I work for them and do a weekly contribution of companionship work as my own respect of the elderly. Home Instead Senior Care was founded fourteen years ago in Omaha, Nebraska. The company by now has grown to eight hundred franchises in twelve countries. I am happy to say that Home Instead provides nonmedical help for the elderly who choose to remain in their homes. Duties are wide-ranging: housekeeping, driving to doctor's appointments, and companionship. Stable labour supply is a problem, as turnover in the senior care industry is high, with entry-level salaries starting around minimum wage. To me, this indicates an imbalance of respect in general. As much as we try to respect the need for elderly care, we pay little respect to those willing to be and stay involved. Again, elder care is confronted with the problems of a pluralistic economic society. If these providers were paying more, then they would need to pass along the costs to their clients. And this calls in competition, as a provider willing to pay more respect to its caregivers could easily be priced out of the market.

Before, within all the industries we have talked about, we have learnt to refer to our workers, labourers, and employees as human resources. Have our elderly become resources to the senior care industry, I wonder? Have they become as anonymous as we all have become in our striving pluralistic economic societies that are not so good anymore? Is that how respect has lost its practitioners?

In the chapters regarding the environment, Mother Nature, planetary systems, and the universe, I pointed out how much our pluralistic economic societies are recently suffering due to the unforeseen forces of nature. Are they, in fact, the unforeseen forces of the inevitable? On a small scale, in our lovely, green New Zealand country, tests carried out by the Hawke's Bay Regional Council showed high concentrations of cyanobacteria, a blue-green algae at the wonderful Lake Tutira. A health warning has come into force, advising people not to swim or pursue other recreational activities which could involve contact with the water until further notice. This was on 10 August, 2011. It was also warned that this lake water should not be used for drinking or cooking purposes. Also, dogs should be kept away from the lake water. Anyone who might come into contact with the lake water could experience severe skin rashes, stomach upsets, hay fever, or asthma attacks. If these symptoms arise, people should immediately contact their general practitioner. Cyanobacteria are an ancient group of organisms, it is said, with characteristics in common with both bacteria and algae. In certain environmental and hydrological conditions, free-floating cyanobacteria cells can multiply and form what are known as algal blooms. Some species produce toxins, which pose a risk to humans and animals alike.

On small and big scales, we are experiencing the power of nature—its ambivalences toward beauty and the beast. On a big scale, major natural catastrophes have dominated a large list of losses in human life as well as in economic figures. Nature's powerhouse is giving us new lessons to understand its might. Five hundred times more energy than the amount in the Haiti quake was released by the earthquake that hit Chile just over a month later. With overall losses of $30 billion (USD) and insured losses of $8 billion (USD), this quake was 2010's most expensive natural catastrophe. Chile is a highly developed country with very strict building codes to take account of the high earthquake exposure. As a result, there were comparatively few human casualties, despite the severity of the quake—the fifth strongest ever measured—although people were, in fact, killed in Chile, too. But it seems that finally, pluralistic economic societies are listening to Mother Nature's call.

Comparatively, in the summer, floods following extreme monsoon rainfall had devastating consequences in Pakistan. For weeks, up to one quarter of the country was flooded. Countless people lost all their worldly possessions. The overall loss totalled $9.5 billion (USD)—an extremely high amount for Pakistan's emerging economy.

Most frequently affected by catastrophes were obviously Asia and America. However, a wide-scale catastrophe also resulted from the heat waves in Russia and neighbouring countries between July and September 2010. Many places, including Moscow, experienced record temperatures. In some regions of central Russia, they exceeded 30^0 Celsius for two months on end. As mentioned before, forests burned. The fires threatened nuclear facilities and areas where the ground had been contaminated by radioactive fallout from Chernobyl. At least 56,000 people died as a result of heat and air pollution, making it the most deadly natural disaster in Russia's history. In this case, I have to add my question: Was this a sole natural disaster, or did some aspects of wanting to thrive under new economic rules add to the outcome in this former communistic country?

Well, the global distribution of natural catastrophes in 2010 was comparable to that of previous years. Most catastrophes occurred on the American continent with a figure of 365 and in Asia with a figure of 310. One hundred twenty natural catastrophes could be recorded in Europe, ninety in Africa, and sixty-five in Australia—respectively, Oceania. North and South America accounted additionally for the largest portion of insured losses, namely around two thirds. Some 17 percent of the losses were incurred in Europe, where the most expensive individual event was the Winter Storm Xynthia, which mainly affected Spain and France, causing overall losses of $6 billion (USD) or €4.5 billion. As is usual with windstorms in Europe, the share of insured losses totalled to an enormous $3 billion (USD) or €3.4 billion in countries that are already struggling to stabilize their Euro.

Natural catastrophes in Australia or Oceania gave rise to 16 percent of global losses. The most costly event was the earthquake of 4 September in Christchurch on New Zealand's most precious South Island. Christchurch was the third largest city of New Zealand, and the earthquake crumbled the CBD down to a war zone. With an additional recession and bankrupting financial institutions, losses in the billions could be added. Australia, due to two further severe hailstorms on top of the droughts and flooding, could count its losses at well over $1 billion (USD) in the month of March 2010.

We can see how fragile our pluralistic societies have become in view of all these unforeseen events we have not yet had the ability to look back at, as nearly all of them are categorized as the first ever witnessed in human history. Now we can look back; the science of Mother Earth's might as well as the miracles of the universe are unprecedented. And now, for the first time in human history, maybe we can start to *respect* the unforeseen. Even the unforeseen does deserve respect—or maybe not even but more likely because of it. After all, the unforeseen is part of existence, as is everything else that matters.

Maybe it is time again to reflect on the power of individuality versus plurality in order to give respect a more doable platform. Our economic societies, with the help of all individuals, could get to the point where respect can fit in with the aim of working and being profitable. Profits can be put towards this practice, which I might name the platform of respect. Rewarding systems could be integrated in all political, social, fiscal, and business structures. Rewarding those who are in the process of respecting existence in its own but simple right could become a mutual conduit for both individual and pluralistic economic societies.

We are, at present, very much at a loss for respectful individuals such as Martin Luther King, Mahatma Gandhi, Albert Schweitzer, or Mother Teresa. I have only come across a few I could truly respect in my nearly sixty-five years of existence, and those were people I admired and respected for their integrity within the work they did.

Yes, I admired Martin Luther King, had a high regard for Gandhi, and read everything about Albert Schweitzer when I was in my teens. Later, I was in the fortunate position to have met Mother Teresa personally. I sensed her wonderful, loving spirit of care and respect.

What caused these people to develop their potential to reach such powerful influence in the world? What moved Martin Luther King to broadcast his vision so clearly that it lasted generations beyond him? What gave Mahatma Gandhi the nerve to hold true to his ideals amidst even the greatest adversity? What enabled Albert Schweitzer to transform his life to humanitarian services on such a big scale? Where did Mother Teresa acquire the determination to give and give with complete surrender to a higher calling?

Was it because they could tap into the hidden powers of their minds, or was it because they stayed true to their individuality? Scientists have concluded that the average person only draws upon 10-20 percent of her or his brainpower. [54] The remainder of this brainpower lies dormant until we get the chance to learn how to develop and strive toward our full potential. I believe that any man can come into his own greatness by increasing knowledge, exercising mental discipline, and generating insightful discoveries that then can be employed to improve his life—and yes, sometimes aid all of humanity. But I also believe that this cannot be achieved with all the attractions a pluralistic economic society constantly has to offer, as they merely draw the focus away from the self of a person. They simply distract everybody, and with that distraction, nobody will come to develop the full potential of their brain power. I also believe it is no coincidence that people like Martin Luther King, Gandhi, Albert Schweitzer, or Mother Teresa lived very recluse lifestyles and shied away from enjoying the so-called pleasures of a pluralistic economic society.

To me, plain existence still is the one and only existence that deserves respect. And in that, we are all included, as I have outlined already. If we have and can carry the Hug Me pillow from Chapter 12 through our lives and maintain the ability to look back at the moment we came into this life, then I truly believe we also are able to maintain our self-respect. With that, we are not in need of any outside, worldly lure. We can greatly increase our ability to be powerful, intelligent, creative, and expressive and will find the way to access reasoning and intuition. Intuition, in my language, is the purest form of self-respect. But intuition lives in individuality and transmits from there to where it's needed.

During my early Gestalt therapy studies, I learnt of Ruth Cohn. Ruth was born in 1912 as a Jew and sadly suffered due to this during the atrocities of WWII and the Holocaust. She nevertheless never left her truth and contributed to society by stimulating personal growth and learning in the midst of life. She was a psychotherapist, educator, and poet. I learnt of her teachings of TCI—theme-centred interaction—and felt high regard for her teachings. TCI showed me how we can teach our children to maintain their individuality and not be overrun by a pious buffet of a pluralistic economic society. I remember, when reading her books, thinking that Ruth was entering utopia and that such education for children never would become possible. Too much effort and money had already gone into child education towards building a generation that would foster deeper and deeper into the demands of our pluralistic and money-driven societies. Back in the 70s, when I learnt of Ruth Cohn, I had already given up hope for a better individualistic future for our children, I admit. But I kept her teachings in my heart.

Ruth had her own pathway of growth. She grew up in Germany, but in 1933, during the Third Reich, she fled to Switzerland, where she was admitted into the University of Zurich. There she studied psychology and minored in pre-clinical medicine and psychiatrics. She completed additional studies in education, theology, literature, and interaction. She is still best known as the creator of TCI. She became the founder of the Workshop Institute for Living Learning (WILL). There is no better word for a training centre of her module. Today the same is known as the Ruth Cohn Institute for TCI. During the first years after the development of TCI, its use grew rapidly in the United States. Those were the years of the 70s through to the 80s where a renaissance towards individuality was very much felt throughout. But soon, as with other individuality-focused programs in the US, TCI became less taught and is virtually unknown in the US today. Yet it continues to be well-known and an important concept for education, therapists, supervisors, and managers in Germany, Switzerland, Austria, Hungary, and India. Whenever I teach, I still mention Ruth Cohn. Her teachings deserve to be respected as much as her memory. Ruth Cohn died in 2010.

Ruth encouraged young school children to be their own chairpeople. In her teachings, it is left to each one to be responsible for her or his own thoughts, feelings, and needs. This requires that a person takes herself or himself seriously as well as take each other seriously. The theme involved in that very moment of time was to display commitment and responsibility for being part of this process. This implies, without further explanations, respecting others in their thoughts, feelings, and needs.

The second most important rule of respect and responsibility is the respect of the here and now. In other words, with Ruth Cohn's teachings, our children would learn that disturbances have precedence. They don't get brushed under the carpet, as in most of our pluralistic economic societies, any disturbance is indeed a mere hindrance towards the so-called desired success. Ruth Cohn's teachings insist that when disturbances are not addressed, they start to occupy energy and prevent people from being in the here and now. At times—most of the times—such unaddressed disturbances become hidden agendas. The idea is at least to give a space to such disturbances, where possible, remedy them, or otherwise agree to consciously park them, but not brush them under the carpet to breed hidden agendas.

Ruth Cohn maintains that we all need a dynamic balance. Therefore, she has placed in equation (for the lack of a better word) the relation between certain components that need to be kept in a dynamic balance for a group to achieve its goals. Recognition of the here and now, mentally and physically, is important in this. The components are the individual—the "I" and the need of the group and the "we," as well as these two placed in perspective with the theme—the mental here and now, the environment, and the physical here and now. This can be any group formation, be it within a family, school class, employment situation, or leisure time event. Within this group dynamic, we have to learn to ensure a balance between moments:

(a) where the theme prevails, or other moments,
(b) where the group dimension prevails, and yet again other times, or
(c) where the individual has a dedicated space to be at the centre of attention.

All this happens in a given context—the globe, your physical here and now—which offers some opportunities and also imposes certain limits. All participants, including a group leader, are expected to contribute to establish, maintain, or contribute to re-establish the dynamic balance at any given moment. This model is very encouraging, as it gives respect to everyone participating, not just the leader of the group, but in addition, also, the very unforseen. Needless to say, it would need practice, as in today's world, we have not been taught to be individually interactive or respect the here and now of any given moment.

To regain the value of individuality, there are eleven important essential life skills to look at. These are your self, self-respect, undivided attention, concentration, memory, listening, imagination, reasoning, intuition, breathing, and entrainment.

Let's start doing our first steps again away from the jungle of conditioned perception. Everything begins and ends with you. When you can view yourself from different perspectives, you will develop a greater awareness of who you are and how to become the person you desire to be. Gaining awareness of how you cause everything in life gives you knowledge, and with that comes the greatest gift of all—the power of knowing how to change. In short, you have gained self-respect.

Attention is one of our greatest commodities! Our teachers in schools are challenged, but they—along with parents—need to teach children to put their whole selves into whatever they are doing. Everybody can relearn to be in the here and now to reap the beauty and fullness of each moment. I encourage teachers and parents alike in this challenge. You will be a great influence on your children when you give your undivided attention, and your children will learn the values of the same in the process.

You will learn that when holding your attention where you want it for as long as you desire will make you powerful, effective, and efficient. A high degree of concentration is one of the secrets to success in the business world, in the field of education, for artists and musicians, and for everyone who wants to understand commitment. Concentration is a skill that can be built with exercise and practice.

You also can learn the skill of drawing out of your brain, at will, what you have stored there. Undivided attention and concentration together build the power of memory. Needless to say, the ability to strengthen memory saves time, produces relaxation, and helps you learn from the past so that you can live a better present and become fully aware of your here and now.

In our pluralistic economic societies, listening skills seem to have vanished completely. Everybody is exhausted by having to listen to their demands. We only have to look at the daily advertising content that is brought to our attention. Our brains can hardly cope with that, and the result is a total collapse of listening skills. Everybody only seems to have become limited to what one wants to hear, not to what is actually said. More than ever, everyone loves to be heard. And there is nothing right or wrong with that. Still, it would be to everybody's benefit if we could learn how to cultivate our ability to listen to our inner selves through meditation. You will achieve the ability to become still-minded and a calming presence for others in your company. Listening to your inner self will also enable you to listen to other people. If you pay yourself respect, then you can pay respect to others. Good listeners are not only great marriage partners, but also wonderful parents, sought-after employees, compassionate friends, and wise counsellors.

There is one skill that distinguishes the exceptional person from the average one, though, and that is the skill of imagination. Are you a parent who sighs when your youngster surprises you with his or her imagination? Don't judge it, and don't sigh. Imagination gives your child the ability to improve himself or herself just by creating new ways of being. It is an excellent skill. Every great discovery in our world was made by someone who could imagine.

Reasoning is another very important skill that should not be underestimated. You may hear yourself saying to your child, "Don't reason with me!" in order to receive immediate respect for an immediate concern. But, dear parent, do listen first. Reasoning skills are built through developing memory, attention, and imagination. Learning to discern cause is, after all, a function of reasoning. A person who reasons well can learn from any experience, produce growth and understanding, and become healthy, wealthy, and wise. So don't disrespect your child when he or she wants to reason. Encourage your son or daughter by using her or his skills of memory, attention, and imagination.

In our world of pluralistic and social economic demands, we have, so it seems, completely forgotten about one aspect of our existence, and that is intuition. We have learnt to reason more than listen to our gut feelings. We need to regain our balance between genuine reasoning and genuine intuition. True intuition, after all, is the direct grasp of truth. Intuition is our ability to draw from the subconscious store of understanding and wisdom—the teaching from within. And yes, even today, intuition still can be cultivated and developed for better decision-making, understanding your dreams, and drawing upon abilities like clairvoyance and telepathy.

In my profession as a psychotherapist, I draw a lot of attention to my clients to the matter of breathing. It is the most important function to stay alive, in the present, and above all, healthy.

Most people don't think of breath as a function of the mind. Yet conscious breathing is the ability to give and receive energy. It can become an entrance and exit modality of our thought patterns. When breathing in, we take in what we need, and when we breathe out, we let go of what we do not need. This way, we can learn to be more balanced, energized, and relaxed. Moreover, we will gain awareness of our self that exists beyond our physical body. Breath is a God-given gift.

Last, but not least, we come to the most important skill to complement our regained individuality. I can promise you that it will not leave you anymore despite the distractions of the pluralistic economic society you are living in. When we coordinate our head and our heart, we become what I call a whole self—an individual. I have mentioned before how I have experienced myself as a tiny particle that is connected and one with the whole universe. This is what happens when we experience the truth that we are all connected with one another energetically as we realize the connection of our outer, physical selves with our inner, spiritual selves. If you ever have such a peak experience, we can say that you have been entrained. Entrainment is possible. Each one of us can cause this state of consciousness on a regular basis with the practice of mental discipline along with the skills practiced that were outlined before. Let's give our next generation a chance to give and receive respect again.

Maybe the world is awakening. The headlines of the month on October 2011 seem to verify this awakening. The Occupy Wall Street movement has close to $300,000 (USD) as well as storage space loaded with donated supplies in lower Manhattan, the news is reporting. Protesters stared down city officials to hang on to their makeshift headquarters, showed their muscle on Sunday 16 October, 2011 with a big Times Square demonstration, and found legions of activists demonstrating in solidarity across the United

Stated and around the word—yes, also in Auckland, New Zealand. The question raised was this: Could this be the peak for loosely-organized protesters united less by a common cause than by revulsion at what they consider unbridled corporate greed? Or are they just getting started? Though driven by individuals, there were naturally signs of confidence, as there were signs of tensions among the demonstrators at Zuccotti Park, the epicentre of the movement that began a month ago. The troubled demonstrators could not agree on things like whether someone could bring in a sleeping bag and showed little sign of uniting on any policy issues. Other protesters wanted the movement to rally around a goal, while others yet again insisted that wasn't the point.

One university student claimed that they were moving fast without a hierarchical structure and lots of gears turning. Egos are always clashing, and that is what democracy offers. Even if protesters were barred from camping in Zucotti Park, as the property owner and city briefly threatened last week, the movement is continuing. Protesters were working with legal experts to identify alternative sites where the risk of getting kicked out would be relatively low. With masses of blankets, pillows, sleeping bags, cans of food, medical supplies, and even oddities such as a box of knitting wool and twenty pairs of swimming goggles to shield protesters from pepper spray, the protest against corporate greed goes on. They shouted, "We are unstoppable!" and "Another world is possible." Some observers called the movement "madness on the streets," as whiffs of marijuana, grungy clothing, and disarray were witnessed. Yet order mainly prevailed over all.

Many of the largest protests on 16 October, 2011 happened in capitalism-strained Europe, where protesters involved in long-running demonstrations against austerity measures declared common cause with the Occupy Wall Street movement. In Rome, hundreds of rioters infiltrated a march by tens of thousands of demonstrators, causing what the mayor estimated was at least €1 million in damage to city property.

And President Barack Obama referred to protests at the dedication of a monument for Martin Luther King, saying the civil rights leader "would want us to challenge the excesses of Wall Street without demonising those who work there."

Reading all this, I asked myself, *Isn't, in fact, this recent corporate, greedy Wall Street movement simply a conscious or subconscious contemporary response to this apparent loss of respect?* Maybe this movement is a mere expression of dissatisfied consumers and personnel resources—that is, dissatisfied human beings—using the conditioned god, money, as an expression of this very loss.

Yes, it seems the individual right to get up and vent is winning over the past times of sitting quietly and letting money rule the world. I guess the critical step still lies ahead of us. We must realize, to a deeper extent, how we can take that awakened emotion towards focusing on what really counts. And if this brings about changed governments, so let it be. Change is the most innate movement of nature, after all. And with that, the answer to my question, "Who deserves respect?" becomes once again an easy one to answer. The answer is that every living matter deserves respect. Everything that exists deserves respect.

In the big picture of existence, we are all one, and yet also "al-one." Our feelings of sometimes standing alone should not lead us away from who we really are to becoming people we are not. I invite everyone to look into their own mirror of conditioned perceptions and ask themselves, "Is this the real me?" If the answer is yes, you have gained self-respect.

Consequently, to whom or what we give our respect and how we give it is our choice. Our choice can be exerted as respectful, as we would like to obtain it on the receiving end of respect.

References, Citations and Recommendations of Literature

*1: kj2000.scripturetext.com/exodus/20.htm

*2: *I and Thou,* Martin Buber

*3: Kahlil Gibran, *The Prophet*

*4: Ayn Rand, academicintegrity.org on fundamental values

*5: en.wikipedia.org/wiki/John_N._Gray

*6: Ury, William. *The third side* New York: Penguin, 2000

*7: wn.com/List_of_environmental_topics

*8: en.wikipedia.org/wiki/Environment_in_the People's_Republic_of_China

*9: en.wikipedia.org/wiki/1999_%C4%B0zmit_earthquake

*10: en.wikipedia.org/wiki/1906_San_Francisco_earthquake

*11: across.co.nz/WorldsWorstDisasters.html

*12 en.wikipedia.org/wiki/List_of_avalanches

*13 en.wikipedia.org/wiki/2004_Indian_Ocean_earthquake

*14 en.wikipedia.org/wiki/July_2006_Java_earthquake

*15 en.wikipedia.org/wiki/2005_Kashmir_earthquake

*16 en.wikipedia.org/wiki/2008_Sichuan_earthquake

*17 en.wikipedia.org/wiki/2010_Chile_earthquake

*18 edition.cnn.com/2011/WORLD/asiapcf/03/13/japan.quake/index.html

*19 en.wikipedia.org/wiki/2011_T%C5%8Dhoku_earthquake_and_tsunami

*20 en.wikipedia.org/wiki/Great_Mississippi_and_Missouri_Rivers_Flood_of_1993

*21 en.wikipedia.org/wiki/1998_Yangtze_River_Floods

*22 en.wikipedia.org/wiki/2000_Mozambique_flood

*23 en.wikipedia.org/wiki/Maharashtra_floods_of_2005

*24 en.wikipedia.org/wiki/2010_Pakistan_floods

*25 emiusa.org/disasterresponse_history.php

*26 en.wikipedia.org/wiki/October_2010_Sumatra_earthquake_and_
tsunami

*27 en.wikipedia.org/wiki/2008_Afghanistan_blizzard

*28 en.wikipedia.org/wiki/Drought_in_Australia#Rainfall_
deficiencies_in_2006

*29 en.wikipedia.org/wiki/Black_Saturday_bushfires

*30 english.gov.cn/2006-08/18/content_364865.htm

*31 en.wikipedia.org/wiki/2003_European_heat_wave

*32 en.wikipedia.org/wiki/2010_Northern_Hemisphere_summer_heat_
wave

*33 en.wikipedia.org/wiki/Tornadoes_of_2011

*34 Wall Street Journal, 28 April 2011, 10.05 P.M. ET: US Tornado
Death Toll Passes 300 / TUSCALOOSA, Al. (AFP)

*35 www.spc.noaa.gov/products/outlook/archive/2011/
day1otlk_20110511_1300.html

*36 en.wikipedia.org/wiki/Black_Death

*37 en.wikipedia.org/wiki/Natural_disaster#Epidemics

*38 en.wikipedia.org/wiki/Famine

*39 en.wikipedia.org/wiki/Tunguska_event

*40 en.wikipedia.org/wiki/Solar_storm_of_1859

*41 www.sciencedaily.com/releases/2001/04/010404081121.htm

*42 www.nasca.org.uk/Strange_Maps/solar/Solar_Flare/solar_flare.html

*43 en.wikipedia.org/wiki/Gamma-ray_burst

*44 en.wikipedia.org/wiki/Kelvin

*45 www.reuters.com/article/2007/11/25/us-britain-climate-oxfam-idU
SL2518480220071125?feedType=RSS&feedName=topNews

*46 en.wikipedia.org/wiki/List_of_religious_populations

*47 www.telegraph.co.uk/news/worldnews/northamerica/usa/8687807/
New-York-beefs-up-World-Trade-Center-site-security-for-
September-11-10th-anniversary.html

*48 in.reuters.com/article/2011/06/29/usa-war-idINN1E75R07C20110629

*49 m o b i l e . r e u t e r s . c o m / a r t i c l e / t o p N e w s / idUSTRE7760G820110809?irpc=932

*50 www.answers.com/topic/john-maynard-keynes-1st-baron-keynes#cite_note-7

*51 Mertens, Steven B.; Flowers, Nancy (May 2003). "Should Middle Grades Students Be Left Alone After School?" (PDF). *Middle School Journal* **34** (5): 57-61.

*52 productivity.stackexchange.com/tags/discipline/info

*53 http://www.globalaging.org/elderrights/us/2008/expands.htm

*54 http://www.som.org/NewPages/Newsite07/SOMNavigation/10ELSkills.html